FOREIGN DOLLAR LOANS
IN EUROPE

FOREIGN
DOLLAR LOANS
IN EUROPE

BY

PAUL EINZIG

Progress in improving the free world's capital markets has become essential if the uninhibited flow of long-term international portfolio capital is not to be a disturbing element in the quest for payments equilibrium.

DOUGLAS DILLON, Secretary of the
U.S. Treasury

LONDON
MACMILLAN & CO LTD
NEW YORK · ST MARTIN'S PRESS
1965

MACMILLAN AND COMPANY LIMITED
St Martin's Street London WC 2
also Bombay Calcutta Madras Melbourne

THE MACMILLAN COMPANY OF CANADA LIMITED
70 Bond Street Toronto 2

ST MARTIN'S PRESS INC
175 Fifth Avenue New York 10 NY

Library of Congress Catalogue Card No. 65 —13616

PRINTED IN GREAT BRITAIN

ONULA

PREFACE

IT is always a fascinating experience to observe how institutional changes come about, and our post-war generation has been fortunate in having lived through that experience in generous measure in the international financial sphere. During the 'fifties and 'sixties new systems, devices and methods have come into existence in that sphere before our very eyes, in answer to challenges offered by difficult and even apparently insoluble problems.

The institutional change which this book aims at describing and analysing is at the time of writing still at a relatively early phase of its evolution. Although a large number of dollar loans were issued in London in 1963–64, and in Continental centres during the late 'fifties and early 'sixties, their volume has not been sufficiently large so far to constitute a factor of an importance comparable to that of the Euro-dollar system — the lending of short- and medium-term dollar deposits in Europe. Quite conceivably the development of the system of issuing long-term dollar bonds in European markets will follow a course similar to that followed by the development of the Euro-dollar market which, ever since its experimental beginnings in 1957, has been expanding almost uninterruptedly until it became a major factor in foreign exchange markets and money markets. It may take, however, some time before the system of European long-term dollar loans could attain a comparable influence.

I am convinced that even if the expansion of the system of issuing dollar bonds, or any foreign bonds in terms of currencies other than that of the country in which they are issued, should be interrupted by some major reverse — as indeed it might well be sooner or later — in the long run it would resume its progress, in the same way as the Euro-dollar system resumed it after each setback. Now that the world of international finance has become familiar with both systems, they are likely to remain an integral part of the international financial mechanism. The change which the advent of the system of issuing dollar bonds outside the United States has brought about is in keeping with the basic trend pointing towards an increasing internationalisation of finance.

Possibly the dollar may not always retain its present prominence as the favourite currency of foreign loan contracts chosen for such transactions in Europe. In fact there have been many loans issued in other foreign currencies and in composite units of account, and these loans have played a part similar to that of European dollar loans, albeit to a lesser degree. But just as Euro-dollars overshadow, and are likely to continue to overshadow in the long run, all other Euro-currencies, so these European dollar bonds are, and are likely to remain in the long run, more important than foreign bonds issued in Europe in other foreign currencies. In any case the operation of the system is substantially the same whether the currency of the loan contracts is the dollar, or some other hard currency, or a composite unit of account, so long as it is not the local currency of the capital market in which the loans are issued. For this reason, our findings could be adapted, with relatively little modification, to a system under which some other currency unit would have for some time at any rate the same prominence as the dollar has at the time of writing.

When the Euro-dollar system drifted into existence during 1957–59 it escaped for a long time the attention of financial commentators (including myself). This history had not repeated itself, and could not possibly repeat itself, in respect of European dollar bonds. From the very outset there was bound to be much more publicity about such transactions than there was until comparatively recently about Euro-dollars. This is only natural. The Euro-dollar market was for years hidden from economists and other readers of the financial Press by a remarkable conspiracy of silence. Bankers deliberately avoided discussing it with financial editors, presumably for fear that publicity might attract additional rivals to the market, or that it might breed criticism in the Press and opposition in official quarters. I stumbled on its existence by sheer accident in

October 1959 — having overlooked, I must confess frankly, a brief article on the subject that appeared in the *Economist* some months earlier — and when I embarked on an inquiry about it in London banking circles several bankers emphatically asked me not to write about the new practice, except perhaps in articles in learned journals or in my books which, they assumed, were in any case too technical for the uninitiated. But it would not have been possible to try to conceal in a similar way dollar bond issues from the wider public. Lending and borrowing of dollar deposits is arranged between foreign exchange departments of banks and foreign exchange brokers on their private telephone lines, with a complete exclusion of publicity. Public issues of bonds, on the other hand, by their very nature, have to be advertised in the Press even if they are not offered for subscription to the general public, and they are necessarily commented upon extensively in the financial columns.

It took something like three years before the Euro-dollar market came to be noticed at all, and even today it does not receive anything like the attention it deserves. It took a further three years before the Central Banks primarily concerned with the practice came to initiate a much-needed exhaustive inquiry, through the medium of the Bank for International Settlements, to ascertain the relevant facts and figures and to analyse their broader implications. Even now, some seven years after dealings in Euro-dollars first became a factor of importance, there is usually a time-lag between changes in the practice and their realisation outside the circle of those directly concerned. And such quotations of Euro-dollar rates as appear in the Press only indicate approximate levels of the rates, not the actual rates at which transactions take place in inter-bank dealings.

On the other hand, facts and figures relating to the practice of issuing foreign dollar loans in Britain and on the Continent are necessarily published in the prospectuses of these issues. Their terms — interest rates, issue prices, redemption dates, etc. — have to be publicised to comply with regulations, even if the whole amounts of the issues had been placed privately in advance of the publication of the prospectuses. The bonds are quoted on Stock Exchanges, even if dealings in them are relatively infrequent. There is a fair amount of current comment on such issues in the financial Press, but they are examined mainly from the point of view of their attractiveness as investments. Admittedly, from time to time financial editors comment on them also from a general technical or economic angle and some of their articles are profound and penetrating. Even so, many fine points of practical or theoretical importance have not been adequately explored, or their position in the system as a whole has not been made clear. Up to the time of writing there has been no systematic attempt — apart from the Report of the U.S. Treasury, *A Description and Analysis of Certain European Capital Markets*, which is largely confined to fact-finding — to present a complete picture of the system and its manifold impact on the national and international economy.

The object of this book is partly to provide factual material and partly to call the attention of economists and of practical experts to the broader implications of the system it describes. I also endeavoured to cover two systems closely related to the issue of European dollar bonds — the system of investment dollars and that of composite units of account. I feel that the space devoted to these subjects calls for no apology.

The change of Government in Britain in October 1964 has introduced an element of uncertainty about the prospects of the market for European dollar bond issues, at any rate as far as London is concerned. Up to the time of writing the new Government has not indicated any intention to adopt exchange restrictions of a kind that would interfere with London's rôle as an entrepôt for foreign capital. But the possibility of such measures cannot be ruled out. Although the placing of foreign bonds with non-resident investors, or even with U.K. investors wishing to replace their existing foreign investments, does not impose any additional burden on the balance of payments, many Socialists are opposed to the practice on the ground of their ideological objections to the maintenance of London's rôle as an international banking centre. They are in favour of relinquishing that rôle because of fears that its fulfilment is liable to conflict with the interests of an expansionary domestic economic policy.

Be that as it may, it must be realised that Britain is not in a position to relinquish that rôle. If my banker did not like my account he could close it by sending me a banker's draft to repay my balance. But how could London repay foreign balances amounting to thousands of millions of pounds out of its dwindling gold reserve that could not be sufficient to cover a fraction of those balances? It is obviously impossible. The large size of foreign holdings of sterling compels London to continue to play the part of a world banker, whether we like it or not. And, that being so, it is to our interest to play that part efficiently. The new device described in this book has contributed towards making London's international banking mechanism more efficient, and for that reason alone it would be a pity to destroy it. But the issuing of foreign dollar bonds through London is well worth maintaining also for the sake of the invisible exports it yields, directly and indirectly, to this country.

In addition to studying the existing literature on the subject, contained mostly in official reports and in financial columns, I endeavoured to ascertain the relevant facts and their interpretations by means of direct inquiries from issuing houses and Stock Exchange firms which are engaged in such transactions mainly in London but also in other financial centres. I sought to obtain the benefit of the views of practical experts on the significance, advantages and disadvantages, limitations and prospects of the new system. I am indeed very much indebted for their generous assistance. Since, however, interpretations and even factual information obtained from various equally authoritative quarters were often contradictory — an experience explained by the fact that no individual, however active, is in a position to have direct knowledge of more than a fraction of the total activity — I had to rely largely on my own judgement when deciding which of the conflicting facts or views I should adopt. Responsibility for my findings is, therefore, entirely my own, and I have no wish to pass on any part of it to those who had helped me, by resorting to the all-too-familiar device of mentioning their names, thereby using their recognised authority for endorsing by implication my statements of fact and my opinions, in spite of disclaiming any intention to do so.

P. E.

120 CLIFFORD'S INN,
  LONDON, E.C.4

November 1964

CONTENTS

CHAPTER 1

INTRODUCTION

THERE is hardly anything new under the sun. Almost every institution, within and without the sphere of the economic system, can be traced to have existed in earlier times, at any rate in some rudimentary form. There are, of course, any number of precedents for dollar loans issued outside the United States before 1914 and again during the inter-war period. Nevertheless, I feel justified in regarding the sudden expansion of the practice of issuing such loans during 1963–64 as an innovation, in the same sense as the acceleration in automation or the expansion of hire purchase after the second World War were institutional development of importance in spite of the existence of both systems in earlier periods. The device of re-depositing dollars outside the United States, too, had existed long before the late 'fifties, but this fact does not affect the revolutionary character of the institutional change caused by the spectacular expansion of the Euro-dollar system in recent years. Likewise, the emergence of a European market for foreign dollar bonds has opened a new chapter in the long history of international capital transactions. Such capital movements have a very extensive literature, and the present volume is confined to one of their special aspects — the issuing of foreign loans in Europe in terms of U.S. dollars or in terms of currency units other than those of the countries where they are issued. It is not concerned with direct investment abroad, or with portfolio investment abroad in the form of loans in the lender's currency or in the form of equities, or with short-term credit transactions unless they arise from the issue of long-term dollar bonds in Europe.

There is no rigid line of demarcation between international money market and international capital market. It would be idle to try to lay down a firm rule about the length of maturity

1

beyond which a loan transaction becomes a capital transaction.
The rule adopted by the United States Treasury in its Report
on *A Description and Analysis of Certain European Capital
Markets*, that any transaction beyond twelve months constitutes
a capital transaction, is not shared either by practical experts
or by economists. Even the more popular textbook-rule, that
credits up to twelve months are short-term transactions, from
one to five years medium-term transactions and over five years
long-term transactions, allows for many exceptions.

A more acceptable rule is that, broadly speaking, the international money market is concerned with self-liquidating
current transactions while the international capital market is
concerned with foreign financing of capital expenditure. In
practice there can be, however, no clear-cut distinction on such
lines. Long-term capital is often borrowed to meet requirements of working capital for the purpose of financing current
transactions — even governments are known to have borrowed
abroad to meet current budgetary deficits — while short-term
credits are often used, by means of repeated renewal, for financing capital expenditure. For our purpose the criterion is whether
funds are raised by means of obtaining some form of bank
credit or by issuing long-term securities.

Loans to foreign borrowers are usually granted in terms of
the lending country's currency. This is only natural. A lending country's currency is almost invariably harder than a
borrowing country's currency. A borrower would not find it
easy to obtain accommodation if he insisted on borrowing
in his own currency, or at any rate the terms on which he
might obtain such loans would be necessarily costly. To
investors in the lending country loans in the borrowing
country's currency would appear unattractive and adequate
response to the issue could only be secured by offering a higher
yield. Since demand for foreign loans almost always exceeds
the amount of capital readily available for that purpose lenders
hold most of the trumps, so that they are usually in a position
to insist on bonds in the denomination of their own currency
or some other currency (or combination of currencies) that
suits their convenience.

2

Introduction

Before the war when some international loans were issued simultaneously in more than one lender country each tranche was usually made in terms of the currency of the country in which it was issued. In some instances these tranches were interchangeable and the bonds were in fact shifted frequently from one country to another through stock arbitrage. Creditors had sometimes the advantage of an option clause under which they were entitled to claim payment of principal and interest in the currency of any of the countries in which there were paying agents to the loan. In many other instances foreign loan contracts included a gold clause guaranteeing the gold value of the payments.

During the 19th century many United States loans were issued in Europe in terms of dollars. In the inter-war period Holland and Switzerland were willing to participate in international loans issued in terms of dollars or sterling instead of insisting on the use of their own currencies for their respective tranches. Moreover, substantial blocks of many European dollar loans issued in New York were usually placed privately in various European markets — not least in London — during periods when public issues of foreign bonds in terms of dollars were under an unofficial but effective ban. In addition, a large proportion of foreign dollar loans issued in New York and originally placed in the United States had the habit of finding their way back gradually to the borrowing country or to some other European country.

The main difference between these precedents and the present practice of issuing dollar loans entirely in Europe lies in the very large proportion of the total foreign borrowing that assumes the latter form. Instead of being occasional transactions, the issue of dollar bonds in Europe has become the prevalent practice. In the past dollar bonds finding their way to Britain, for instance, constituted a mere fraction of foreign loans issued in London in terms of sterling. The same was true more or less about other European markets. From the late 'fifties, however, a very high proportion of continental issues of foreign loans came to assume the form of dollar bonds, and from the middle of 1963 they came to constitute the large majority of foreign loans issued in London.

3

It is probably for the first time that issues of foreign dollar bonds in Europe have assumed sufficiently large proportions to make it necessary to envisage them as a factor liable to affect foreign exchange markets and money markets in a way that differs in some essential respects from the effects of foreign issues made in terms of the currencies of the countries in whose capital markets they are issued. Although at the time of writing the actual importance of that factor is relatively small, it appears possible and even probable that sooner or later it will confront those in charge of monetary policy in general, and foreign exchange policy in particular, with a new set of problems.

Up to now the actual specific effects of European dollar bond issues, as distinct from the general effects of lending abroad, have not yet become sufficiently pronounced to enable us to reach any very definite conclusions about the broader problems involved. The analysis of the system is bound to be, therefore, largely a theoretical exercise whose conclusions might have to be revised in the light of subsequent experience. That is no reason, however, for abstaining from attempting at this early stage to examine the highly complicated cross-currents set into motion by European dollar bond issuing activity. The reciprocal effects of trends of interest rates in this international capital market and those of national interest structure call for particularly close preliminary analysis.

Our first step is to study the background to the development of the new practice. In the next chapter an attempt is made to list the requirements of a good capital market in general and the specific requirements of a good capital market for foreign loans in particular.

Such a preliminary survey is essential in order to enable us to appreciate the significance of the changes that have made it necessary to resort to the new device of issuing loans in terms of a foreign currency. Chapter 3 describes the extent to which the requirements of good capital markets, as defined in Chapter 2, had existed before the first World War and also during the inter-war period, while Chapter 4 indicates the major changes that have occurred in their respect during the post-war period. It will be seen that the international capital market, which operated reasonably efficiently until it broke down during the series of crises of the 'thirties. It was unable in Europe simply to resume in the 'fifties where it had left off a quarter of a century earlier. This was particularly so concerning London.

Chapter 5 indicates the solution resorted to by the London market in an effort to make up for its own deficiencies as well as the deficiencies of the Continental markets, by means of assuming the rôle of an entrepôt for foreign capital. An attempt is made to list the special requirements that are called for in order that such a market should function satisfactorily.

The practice that has actually developed is familiar to relatively few people outside those directly concerned. It is described in some detail in Chapter 6, which deals with problems such as the types of investors interested in the bonds, the composition of issuing consortia and underwriting syndicates which handle such transactions, the discrepancies between the terms of the various issues, the types of borrowers making use of the new facilities, etc.

The international structure of long-term interest rates that has emerged from its operation is analysed in Chapter 7. It bears some similarity to the international structure of short-term interest rates that have developed in the Euro-dollar market and in other Euro-currency markets. An attempt is made here to sort out the multitude of influences affecting the level and trend of these international interest rates, and especially to ascertain the extent to which they are affected by interest rates in the United States.

The sphere in which the impact of European dollar bond issues is the most evident is that of the Euro-dollar market. The relationship is extremely involved and an attempt is made to analyse it in detail in Chapter 8.

Chapter 9 examines the impact of European dollar bond issues on foreign exchanges. This impact is, if anything, even more involved than that of dollar bond issues on Euro-dollar rates. Anyone who hopes to find a short answer to the important question of how these issues affect the dollar will see from this chapter that it all depends on how the dollars are provided for the loans and how the borrowers use the proceeds.

The following chapter deals with the impact of dollar bond issues on domestic interest rates in the United States, in lending countries, in intermediary countries and in borrowing countries. It will be seen that those impacts are manifold and some of them are potentially far-reaching.

While foreign loans issued in European markets in terms of U.S. dollars have been the most popular among the solutions chosen, alternative solutions have also been tried or suggested. Outstanding amongst them is the experiment of issuing foreign loans in terms of composite units of account. That system, which has found fairly widespread application, is examined in some detail in Chapter 11.

The next chapter is devoted to the market in investment dollars, the currency which U.K. residents have to use if they wish to subscribe to European dollar bond issues or to acquire any foreign securities. Even though at the time of writing the high premium on investment dollar bonds prevents their frequent use for that purpose, I deemed it necessary to deal with the system at some length, not so much on account of its present bearing on our main subject as owing to its potential importance. I seized the opportunity for embarking on a much-needed analysis of this little-known interesting market.

Some additional broader implications of the subject are dealt with in Chapter 13. Among others, the question whether European dollar bond issues increase international liquidity or whether they consolidate fluid dollar balances will be examined. An answer is sought on the question whether they have an equilibrating or disequilibrating effect on the balance of payments and whether their effect on the internationalisation of finance is on balance an advantage or a disadvantage.

In the concluding chapter a prognosis is made about the future development of the system. The possibilities of its eclipse through various conceivable influences are examined, and the probable trend of its further progress is sought to be forecast. Whatever the future may hold, it is certain that the new device has, to date, serviced a useful purpose. The formula chosen by the European capital markets — to issue foreign loans in terms of dollars — has gone a long way towards assisting in the revival of foreign issuing activities. While there is room for two opinions about the highly controversial question whether the development and expansion of the Euro-dollar system has been beneficial on balance, it is incontestable that during the brief period of its operation the advantages of issuing activity in European dollar bonds greatly outweigh its disadvantages.

CHAPTER 2

REQUIREMENTS OF CAPITAL MARKETS

ALTHOUGH international capital movements have an extensive literature, no systematic effort seems to have been made to codify the rules defining the requirements of a good market for the issue of foreign loans. Books published on capital markets before the war or since devote most of their attention to the theory of international capital movements in their relation to the balance of payments, or they describe in detail the London capital market without displaying any special interest in foreign issuing activity. In my book *The Fight for Financial Supremacy*, published in 1931, I sought to compare the facilities of London, New York, Paris, Amsterdam and Switzerland for the issue of foreign bonds. A report published shortly before the war by the Royal Institute of International Affairs examines in some detail the conditions in which financial centres can fulfil that function satisfactorily. It is confined, however, to an examination of the three principal capital markets of the inter-war period and it was only interested in certain aspects of the subject. Nor have other books listed in our Bibliography covered the theoretical or practical problems of international bond issues in adequate detail. A book published by the *Neue Zürcher Zeitung* in 1959, covered a wide range of financial centres, and its practical material was up to date, but it was factual rather than analytical.

By far the most useful publication, from the point with which we are here concerned, is the Report of the United States Treasury, *A Description and Analysis of Certain European Capital Markets*, to which reference was made in the last chapter. It deals with some half-dozen capital markets and contains a wealth of relevant factual material, reinforced by statistical tables, which lends itself for serving as a basis of compari-

8

son between the relative merits of the various markets. It provides excellent raw material to enable us to elaborate for ourselves a set of rules on the requirements of markets for foreign issues. The present attempt to codify the rules of international capital markets is based extensively, but by no means exclusively, on that excellent material.

It is necessary to discriminate between requirements of capital markets according to whether the new issues floated in it are for domestic or foreign borrowers, according to whether the loans which are issued for foreign borrowers are in terms of the currency of the issuing market or in some other unit, and according to whether the loans are taken up by residents or non-residents in the issuing country.

The rules applicable to capital markets whose function is confined to that of entrepôt of foreign capital will be examined in Chapter 5. The present chapter undertakes the examination of the requirements of a capital market for issues, domestic or foreign, taken up by investors in the countries of the financial centres which handle these issues. From an international financial point of view the capacity of capital markets to absorb domestic issues is of considerable importance in that such markets reduce the demand which would otherwise compete for the resources of foreign financial centres.

In many respects there is no difference between the conditions that a capital market has to fulfil in order to function satisfactory in respect of domestic capital issues and in respect of foreign capital issues. The following are the general requirements that a good market for long-term capital issues, whether for domestic or for foreign purposes, have to fulfil:

(1) It must have plentiful supplies of accumulated capital available, with an ample and continuous stream of new supplies to replenish its resources.

(2) There must be an investing public in the country concerned able and willing to absorb large amounts of new issues.

(3) It must possess financial houses that are experienced in handling capital issues and inspire confidence among investors.

9

(4) It must have adequate numbers of financial institutions which are able and willing to underwrite capital issues.

(5) Credit facilities must be freely available for issuing houses and underwriters that handle capital issues, pending the absorption of such issues by the investing public.

(6) Adequate information on the capital issue must be available to subscribers and investors.

(7) There must be a reasonable degree of competition between issuing houses, also between underwriters.

(8) The currency in terms of which the securities are issued must inspire a reasonable degree of confidence.

(9) Economic conditions in the country in which the issues are made must be reasonably stable.

(10) Political conditions and prospects in that country must inspire a reasonable degree of confidence.

(11) There must be an adequate number of creditworthy borrowers wanting to avail themselves of the facilities offered by market.

(12) The level of interest rates must be such as to be acceptable to borrowers of good standing.

(13) The issuing centre must possess a good Stock Exchange with a reasonably large turnover in the types of securities issued.

(14) There must be no ban, official or unofficial, on new issues.

(15) There must be no excessive official interference with new issues, aimed at securing absolute priority for certain types of investment.

(16) There must be no excessive official borrowing that would drain the market's capital resources.

(17) Stamp duties on new issues and on transfers of securities when they change hands subsequently must not be too high.

(18) Other costs of new issues must not be excessive.

(19) Taxation on personal investment incomes and on corporation incomes must not be excessive.

(20) Monetary policy must not cause or tolerate undue instability in the market for long-term loans.

Requirements of Capital Markets

The basic condition of a capital market is the existence of adequate supplies of capital. That is the reason why countries with otherwise advanced economies do not always possess good capital markets. For instance, although Germany was between the wars one of the most highly developed countries, the wholesale destruction of her capital resources by inflation after the first World War made it impossible for her to cover her domestic capital requirements during the 'twenties. To give a more recent instance, although the industrialisation of Italy and Japan has reached an advanced stage and they have a highly developed system of banking, the inadequacy of their accumulated savings has so far prevented them from developing capital markets capable of meeting their domestic capital requirements in full, let along contributing towards meeting requirements of other countries. It is of course conceivable that a capital market without adequate domestic financial resources of its own is able to borrow abroad extensively and to re-lend borrowed capital to domestic or foreign borrowers.

The Report of the United States Treasury on European capital markets provides a mass of factual and statistical material on the savings available in the capital markets of the Western European countries it covers. Each chapter dealing with individual countries examines closely the amount of such savings by individuals, business firms and Government departments. The capital available for new issues may assume the form of liquid assets accumulated by the private sector of the economy — individual investors, business firms, insurance companies, investment trusts and unit trusts, family trusts, charitable trusts, pension funds, etc. — or they may be owned by the public sector — reserves of pension and national insurance funds, assets of savings banks, funds handled by the Public Trustee, etc.

Even the most plentiful supplies of accumulated savings are not inexhaustible. Growing economies and steadily rising prices mean ever-increasing capital requirements, and they can only be met out of a steadily increasing stream of new savings, both personal and institutional. No capital market can survive if it has to rely solely on past savings because the rate of replacement

11

of its capital resources is kept down unduly by over-consumption or high taxation.

In itself the mere existence of liquid resources available for investment in new issues would not be sufficient to ensure their success unless those owning or controlling the resources are actively interested in the type of investment these issues represent. If those with whom the decisions rest are not accustomed to invest in long-term securities, or if they are prevented by legal or conventional inhibitions to acquire such securities, or if for some reasons, whether general or specific, they have no confidence in them, no capital market can develop. This is one of the main reasons why the capacity of the French and German capital markets to absorb bond issues bears no relation to the high degree of development of their financial systems or to the volume of their financial resources.

In some countries savings assume mainly the form of hoarded gold or notes, or savers may prefer to retain their liquidity by keeping their savings in the form of bank deposits or savings-bank deposits. Banks which hold their savings may not be in the habit of investing in long-term securities outside the gilt-edged market. Disastrous experience such as that of the German victims of inflation, or that of the French victims of both inflation and wholesale defaults by foreign borrowers, is liable to discourage individual investors from acquiring long-term securities. In such situations capital markets depend largely on institutional investors and public investors. In any case, all modern capital markets have in fact come to depend to a large and increasing extent on such investors rather than on the multitude of individual investors, though the latter still play a sufficiently important part to influence to a large degree the capacity of the capital market to absorb large and frequent capital issues systematically.

In addition to the employment of new savings in new issues they are also acquired with the aid of funds raised through realising existing investments. Such turning over of investments is usually practised on a fairly large scale. But markets for new issues cannot in the long run depend for their sole or main source of capital on the investors' willingness to switch

their investments. In any case the process entails a depreciation of existing securities, sold out for the sake of being able to
reinvest the proceeds, and if this occurs systematically over a
period it is liable to discourage demand for new issues. At any
rate, it raises their interest rates, since they are influenced by
the yields obtainable on existing securities.

The possession of large capital resources and the willingness
of their owners to invest in long-term securities would be of
limited use if the market did not also possess efficient institutions capable of collecting these resources from willing investors
and passing them on to those who want to borrow them. The
actual mechanism that fulfils this function varies from country
to country.

Under the American system the banking group that handles
the issue includes a very large number of financial houses each
of which takes over an agreed proportion of the amount available
and is directly responsible for placing its share with investors.
Bondsellers who pay visits to potential buyers play an important
part in the placing of new issues, and a very high proportion
of the bonds find their way to the public through sales over
the counter of the issuing banks.

Under the traditional British system two sets, and possibly
three sets, of financial houses are engaged in the operation. The
issues are floated by one single issuing house, or a very small
number of issuing houses. There is, in addition, a syndicate of
underwriters who are not required to handle the issue in the
first instance, and may not be called upon to handle it at all
even at a later stage, but merely assume between them the risk
that the issue may not be covered in full by applications of
subscribers. If the loan is covered their function ceases. It is
only if the loan is not covered fully that underwriters have to
take over their percentage of the amount left uncovered, and
they then become responsible for placing it with investors.
There may be a third set of institutions, the sub-underwriters
who relieve underwriters of part of the risk that the latter had
assumed. Members of this group are usually large investors
who are prepared to keep the securities as part of their port-
folios, or stockbrokers who can depend on receiving a number of

applications for the issue from their regular customer.

In France new issues are placed to a large degree by means of sales over the counter by banks. For this reason the participation in every issuing group of a commercial bank possessing many branches is considered essential to ensure the success of the operation.

What really matters is that there should be a sufficiently large number of financially strong firms able and willing to carry loans which cannot be placed with investors immediately, and to wait until the market has settled down sufficiently to enable them to unload gradually their holdings without forcing down the price. The number of participating firms and their total resources available for that purpose must be sufficiently large to enable them to absorb and carry fairly substantial amounts of such 'undigested' issues, so that the market does not become hopelessly congested as a result of partial failures of a few issues.

Public issues are highly involved operations calling for a great deal of technical knowledge of accountancy, law, publicity, Stock Exchange technique, etc. In order to be able to judge the debtor's capacity to pay, issuing houses must be qualified to assess his financial position and prospects, also the economic background on which his position is conditioned in the long run. They must also be well informed about political conditions and prospects in the borrower's country and in the world at large.

It is also essential that the banking houses engaged in such operations should enjoy high prestige and should inspire confidence among the investing public. Their name should be of such a high standing that its presence on the prospectus should in itself go a long way towards ensuring the success of the operation. To that end it is important that the past record of issuing houses should be good. It is true, issuing houses have no legal responsibility for the losses suffered by investors through defaults by debtors on bonds issued by them. Nevertheless, it is to their interest to select with great care the transactions they handle and to avoid as far as possible risking such defaults, each of which is likely to be remembered against them on future occasions, unless the defaults were due to some unpredictable *force majeure* over which the debtors had no control, such as a world war. It is to the interest of issuing houses to scrutinise the proposed transactions with the utmost care and to satisfy themselves as far as this is humanly possible that the debtors are likely to be both willing and able to meet their engagements.

Houses of good standing are indeed short-sighted if they handle loans for debtors with a bad record or with unpromising prospects. They might earn an immediate profit on such transactions, but this is liable to be paid for dearly in the long run by a deterioration of the goodwill represented by the confidence the investing public have in their judgement. Should, contrary to their expectations, a formerly reliable borrower default, houses of first-rate standing always deem it to be their foremost duty to investors as well as in accordance with their own interests to bring the utmost pressure to bear on the defaulters to induce them to meet their liabilities. Failing that, they must use their influence in their own centres and in foreign centres to ensure that the defaulters should be blacklisted until they have come to an arrangement with their existing creditors.

It is essential that a good capital market should possess adequate short-term credit facilities at reasonably low interest rates, enabling issuing houses and underwriters to carry temporarily amounts of loans not taken up by the public. The British system under which the functions of issuing houses are separated from those of commercial banks enables the former and their underwriting syndicates to draw temporarily upon the credit resources of the latter. The development of the Eurodollar system under which banks and other institutions of good standing are able to borrow large amounts at short notice has greatly assisted the capital markets in respect of securing funds for the provisional financing of bond issues.

Investors may be reluctant to risk their capital by subscribing to new issues unless they can depend on being able to obtain subsequently reliable and prompt information relevant to the position and prospects of their investment. In itself the publication of the flood of information contained in prospectuses of new issues and the publicity campaign that accompanies them is not sufficient. In the long run it is to the interest of the

development and maintenance of good market for new issues
that there should be a reliable, well-informed and independent
financial Press that is capable of keeping investors up to date
with the latest developments liable to affect their investments, and that is prepared to comment on them fearlessly.
Not unnaturally banks are inclined to prefer a subservient
financial Press which confines itself to publication of items
released or approved by them. Taking a long view, however, they are likely to find it easier to float new issues if the
investing public can also depend on obtaining reliable information independently of officially-inspired material, both at the
time of the new issues and subsequently.

The Report of the United States Treasury stresses the need
for competition between issuing houses as one of the major
conditions of a good capital market. This attitude appears to
indicate that the Report was compiled by experts belonging
essentially to the post-war generation. Anyone who remem-
bers the excesses of competition for foreign loans by issuing
houses during the 'twenties is bound to realise that competition
need not necessarily be an unqualified blessing. Beyond doubt
a quasi-monopolistic position occupied by issuing houses provides temptation and opportunity for misusing it. But there
is another side to it. During the years that preceded the Wall
Street slump there was an overdose of competition between
relatively inexperienced New York issuing houses. As a result
many would-be borrowers in Central Europe and elsewhere were
inundated with competitive offers and were enabled to borrow
excessive amounts on terms which had failed to allow for the
extent of the risk involved. Nor was the rule that defaulters
must not be allowed to borrow unless they have come to terms
with their creditors observed too strictly by the over-eager
would-be lenders.

Absence of competition need not necessarily be disadvan-
tageous from the point of view of a good capital market.
Under a long-established tradition of the London banking community, issuing houses specialised in certain countries before the
war, and never, or hardly ever, poached on each other's preserves. This did not mean that they were in a monopolistic

position, for rival offers to borrowers by American and Continental issuing houses kept their terms reasonably competitive in spite of the almost complete absence of competition in London itself.

Nor is the existence of permanent underwriting arrangements by which underwriting syndicates consist of permanent members participating in new issues at an agreed proportion any disadvantage. So long as such arrangements are not misused they can do little harm to offset the advantages offered by such a steady system.

One of the main reasons why investors are apt to distrust issues with fixed interest rates is distrust in the stability of the currency of the loan contract. Apart altogether from periodically recurrent acute devaluation scares, creeping inflation tends to discourage investors from holding fixed interest-bearing securities, because it gradually reduces the purchasing power of the currency in which they are to receive interest and capital repayment. This distrust may find expression in the terms which are acceptable to subscribers. But once investors become really inflation-conscious they might require such a high yield that borrowers of standing might be unwilling to meet them. A reasonable degree of the stability, both external and internal, of the currency of the loan contract is, therefore, one of the basic requirements of a good capital market.

Economic instability in the lending country is liable to react unfavourably on its capital market, inasmuch as it inspires distrust among investors. Unsound Budgetary policies in lending countries, apart altogether from their inflationary effect, tend to discourage investors from subscribing to bonds because of the anticipation of heavy Government borrowing that is liable to raise long-term interest rates and to compete with private issues.

Domestic or international political uncertainty, or the fear of the advent of a régime hostile to investors, tend to operate in the same sense. That is one of the reasons why, within their quantitative limitations, the Swiss and Dutch capital markets compare favourably in many ways with other capital markets.

Uncertainties, whether political, financial or economic, that

17

are liable to affect the borrowers' ability or willingness to meet their liabilities constitute one of the major obstacles to the development of active markets in foreign issues. During the 'thirties and again during the early post-war years, very few foreign borrowers were looked upon as being sufficiently credit-worthy to inspire confidence among issuing houses, underwriters and investors. Even in the 'sixties the number of those who pass muster is relatively small, though it is sufficient to ensure an active issue market.

Reference was made above to the possibility of circumstances in which potential borrowers of high standing are unwilling to pay sufficiently high interest rates to induce investors to sub-scribe. Considerations of prestige deter first-rate borrowers from paying interest rates which had been charged to second-rate borrowers in the past. Interest rates are liable to become prohibitive in this sense for reasons other than inflation. If general demand for capital exceeds supply considerably interest rates are liable to rise to a level at which demand by good-class borrowers becomes automatically discouraged. During periods of inflation, however, many industrial borrowers who stand to benefit by the rising trend of prices are apt to disregard high interest rates, owing to their ability to pass on the additional cost they represent. Rising or high interest rates are not, therefore, an absolute obstacle to the maintenance of an active new issue market.

In order to ensure a steady interest of investors in new issues they must have the assurance that they are able to realise their securities easily and at competitive prices whenever they feel inclined to do so. That end is assured if the securities are listed on a good Stock Exchange. The larger is the turnover the lower is the cost of transferring stocks to other investors, because in a wide market it is easy to find a counterpart for a large buy-ing or selling order without moving the price unduly against the buyer or the seller who takes the initiative. One of the great advantages of New York lies in the immensity of its turnover.

Freedom from official restrictions, statutory or otherwise, on new issues is an important condition. But the need to apply for licence to authorise individual issues need not in itself unduly handicap a capital market, provided that the authorities are reasonably liberal in granting such licenses. Nor is official co-ordination of public issues in order to avoid a rush by borrowers that would cause a congestion of the market, by itself an obstacle.

Over-spending by the Government or by local authorities is liable to be detrimental to the development of a good capital market for private borrowers, not only because it tends to raise interest rates but also because the priority that official borrowing is apt to be given, officially or otherwise, tends to drain the market of resources available for other purposes.

If the authorities lay down a too rigid list of priorities among non-official borrowers it may effectively prevent access to the market by borrowers with a low priority. Even a *de facto* priority, such as enjoyed by borrowing for building purposes in Germany, is apt to handicap the development of a good capital market for other borrowers.

Unduly high stamp duties on new issues, by raising the cost of such transactions, tend to discourage them. If the demand is sufficiently strong, however, borrowers are willing to pay this once-for-all expense, unless they are able to find alternative markets where the cost of new issues is lower, or unless they find alternative ways of covering their capital requirements. The attitude of investors is liable to be influenced also by the high cost of subsequent transfers of securities. They expect borrowers to make the terms of the issues sufficiently attractive to compensate them for that cost, although if the duty is payable by the buyer and not by the seller of the securities its effect on the attitude of subscribers to new issues may not be too pronounced. In the case of bearer bonds transfer tax does not arise, but in some countries a once-for-all levy is payable when they are issued.

Costs other than stamp duties connected with new issues — publicity expenses, legal expenses, accountants' fees, etc. — are liable to affect the efficiency of new issue markets. A widening of the spread between the annual cost of the loans to borrowers and the yield to lenders tends to discourage both parties. Lenders are certain to insist on terms which secure for them the net yield they feel they are entitled to receive to make the investment worth their while.

A high general level of taxation on investment incomes of individuals or corporations is also apt to discourage activity in capital markets. If their taxed income from the investment is too low they may feel it is not worth their while to take the risk involved in investing for the sake of such inadequate return. For this reason capital markets in a country with a relatively low level of taxation on investment incomes are at an advantage over the capital market of a country with a higher level of taxation. The latter is likely to confine its lendings to highly creditworthy borrowers, as their taxed yield on even moderately speculative bonds would not compensate them adequately for the risk involved.

Last but by no means least, it is an essential condition of a good capital market that the prices of bonds should not fluctuate unduly as a result of monetary policy measures. Speculative risk resulting from violent ups and downs of securities caused by such measures is liable to discourage demand for new issues, unless their terms are sufficiently favourable to investors to compensate them for such risk. Under the conception that prevailed until quite recently it was considered to be outside the scope of monetary policy, as distinct from debt management policy, to interfere with the trend of bond prices. According to the new conception developed under the influence of the Radcliffe Report and the American Report on Money and Credit, monetary policy has to aim, however, at influencing the entire structure of interest rates instead of confining itself to influencing short-term interest rates only. This new policy is still in its infancy, but it seems conceivable that its development might affect the facilities of capital markets unfavourably if unexpected changes in monetary policy should exaggerate the effects of changes in short-term interest rates on the trend of bond prices.

All the above requirements apply to markets for domestic as well as foreign issues. There are, however, a number of additional requirements which are peculiar to markets for the issue of foreign securities :

(1) The country of the issuing market must have a favourable balance of payments.

(2) The currency of that country must not be regarded by borrowers as one involving the risk of a revaluation.

(3) It must not be regarded by investors as involving a risk of devaluation.

(4) Domestic requirements enjoying *de jure* or *de facto* priority must not absorb an unduly large proportion of the capital resources available.

(5) There must be no ban on foreign issues or even an unduly restrictive licensing system.

(6) The currency of the lending country must not be subject to exchange restrictions of the kind that would prevent or gravely handicap the issue of foreign securities or subsequent dealings in them.

(7) It is an advantage if the issuing centre has a good foreign exchange market.

(8) It is an advantage if the issuing centre has good facilities for the short-term investment of the proceeds of foreign loans by borrowers.

The efficiency of a capital market, even for purely domestic issues, is liable to be affected by the state of the balance of payments. It is liable to affect decisively the ability and willingness of lending countries to lend abroad. Taking a long view, it is essential for such countries to have a reasonably steady export surplus which, unless lent abroad in the form of long-term loans, would assume the form of additional short-term claims or would lead to an increase of the gold reserve.

Although this may now appear beyond controversy, not so very long ago the opposite view — that a country which lends abroad in excess of its export surplus is in a position automatically to increase its export surplus as a result of such overlending — was firmly held by many economists in Britain. It was a quasi-religious belief, based on Britain's favourable experience during the 19th century when her balance of payments position was so strong that she could safely overlend on the firm assumption that sooner or later the amount overlent would come to be spent on British goods or services. The unofficial embargo on foreign loans imposed during the 'twenties had been strongly opposed on the basis of pre-1914 experience, in total disregard of the change in Britain's fundamental situation. The reason why Britain had been safe in overlending before 1914 was that her goods had been competitive. After 1918 she was no longer safe in overlending because, with sterling overvalued, her goods were no longer sufficiently competitive, and because meanwhile structural changes developed to her detriment. In the changed circumstances overlending tended to result in a decline of her gold reserve and/or an accumulation of her foreign short-term indebtedness.

Amidst conditions prevailing between the wars, and again since the second World War, Britain had to cut her coat according to her cloth, instead of assuming that the cloth would be forthcoming in the required length regardless of the way in which her coat was cut. She could only afford to issue foreign long-term loans to the extent of the surplus of her balance of payments. Disregard of the rule carried its penalty in the form of pressure on sterling and loss of gold which she could ill afford to lose.

In practice the rule need not apply rigidly to every single year. If a country has a large gold reserve or if it is in a position to attract short-term balances easily it is able to grant long-term loans abroad over a number of years even if it has no correspondingly favourable trade balance available for that purpose. This is what happened in the United States during the late 'fifties and early 'sixties. Year after year the New York market handled large foreign issues, even though the balance of payments was persistently unfavourable. Unlike Britain during the 'twenties, however, the United States in the 'fifties was in a strong enough position to be able to afford a decline in her gold reserve and an increase in her short-term liabilities resulting from long-term overlending.

A capital market for foreign loans is not satisfactory unless the country concerned is able to meet temporary ups and downs of its balance of payments, as distinct from a perennial deficit, without having to resort to measures leading on each occasion to a drastic curtailment of foreign long-term borrowing.

While from the lenders' point of view it is essential that the currency of the transaction does not involve a devaluation risk, from the borrowers' point of view it is equally important that it does not involve a revaluation risk. First-rate borrowers who are in a position to say 'no' would only be prepared to borrow in a currency which is liable to appreciate if they could do so on very favourable terms. Likewise, if the currency of the loan contract is liable to depreciate investors are reluctant to hold such loans unless their yield is sufficiently high to make it appear worth their while to take the risk.

From time to time most currencies are bound to be suspected of involving either the risk of devaluation or the risk of revaluation. The situation and prospects of a currency are liable to change with disconcerting suddenness, and seldom is a currency entirely above suspicion from the point of view of both potential borrowers and potential lenders for any length of time. But in the prolonged absence of acute devaluation scares or revaluation scares certain currencies may become reasonably acceptable to both parties.

From the point of view of foreign issuing activity it is essential that there should be enough capital resources for domestic as well as foreign requirements. Otherwise, even in the absence of official priorities in favour of domestic borrowers, pressure of domestic demand might raise long-term interest rates to a level at which it ceases to be attractive to foreign borrowers. In some countries, moreover, domestic requirements of certain categories have an admitted prior claim for capital resources, in which case the possibility of developing a foreign loan market depends on the existence of surplus resources in excess of those earmarked for domestic requirements.

The absence of exchange restrictions of a kind that would prevent their issue is an essential requirement of a market for foreign loans. Under controlled exchange the granting of permits to issue foreign loans may be determined not only by priorities of domestic capital requirements but also by foreign exchange considerations.

It is an advantage if the lending country has a good foreign exchange market which would enable the debtor to withdraw the proceeds of a loan as and when required, to sell forward those portions of the loan which are to be transferred later, and to cover the amounts required subsequently for interest payments and capital repayments in a way that is most convenient. This is not indispensable, however, so long as there are no exchange restrictions to prevent the borrower from selling the proceeds of the loan in some other market, or from surrendering them to the monetary authorities of his own country. The existence of good money market facilities that enable borrowers to employ temporarily the proceeds of the loan pending their transfer is also an advantage.

Foreign issuing activity is stimulated by the existence of a buyers' market in the goods exported by the lending country. If such goods have a sellers' market the exporting country need not go out of its way to increase its exports by granting long-term loans to the importing countries. Difficulties in finding markets abroad tend to induce industries and their Governments to offer such loan facilities as an inducement to importing countries to buy their goods.

CHAPTER 3

PRE-WAR MARKETS IN FOREIGN ISSUES

THIS chapter deals with describing the extent to which the requirements of a good capital market for foreign issues, as enumerated in the last chapter, had existed before the first World War and during the inter-war period. It is always tempting to look back upon past periods with nostalgia and to regard them as pictures of perfection by comparison with the less satisfactory state of affairs prevailing in more recent times. Our difficulties of yesterday are of course never as difficult as our difficulties of today. But even allowing for this, there can be no doubt that in this instance our nostalgia is justified. The international capital markets of the 19th century and of the early 20th century had their shortcomings and had been subject to much criticism in contemporary financial literature. Nevertheless, in this case the picture of near-perfection which we conjure up when glancing back on those days is substantially correct, at any rate in a relative sense. The leading capital markets of the day — London, Paris and Berlin, and later New York — had conformed to ideal requirements to a degree which in our days may well appear to us to be bordering on the unattainable.

To what extent did European capital markets conform to the requirements of a good market enumerated in the last chapter before the first World War ? London and other capital markets had, generally speaking, plentiful supplies of funds available for investment. In the prolonged absence of major wars and amidst conditions of economic and political stability prevailing most of the time, savings were accumulating very satisfactorily. Throughout the 19th century and up to the first World War saving was generally looked upon as one of the major civic virtues. Keynes's immortal remark that 'after all, even a rich man may enter the Kingdom of Heaven if only he saved', truly expressed the prevailing attitude. There was not only willingness but also ample opportunity for saving. Distribution of wealth and income was unequal to a high degree — and, in accordance with the elementary principles of Keynesian economics, this meant that a high proportion of it could be saved. Nor did Governments mop up for their own requirements the funds available through saving. Generally speaking, budgets were balanced, at any rate in the leading countries possessing capital markets. In Britain the public debt was £656 million in 1914 compared with its peak figure of £848 million reached as a result of the Napoleonic Wars — an actual reduction by nearly £200 million between the end of those wars and the beginning of the first World War. Accumulated savings were left at the disposal of private enterprise at home and abroad, and of foreign Governments in need of loans.

There was in each of the principal lending centres, and also in smaller countries such as Holland, Switzerland, Belgium and Sweden, an investing public accustomed to subscribe to foreign bond issues and it was encouraged to do so by the stable monetary conditions prevailing between the battle of Waterloo and the first battle of the Marne. During earlier centuries borrowers had depended mainly on loans from powerful banking firms, but by the second half of the 19th century and even more the early part of the 20th century the broader investing public came to be able and willing to participate extensively in such transactions and to supply the bulk of the capital required. Their combined resources exceeded considerably any conceivable amounts that even the richest banking houses, or any combination of them, would have been able to lend.

The capital markets were well served by banks experienced in the art of issuing securities. In addition to old-established merchant banking firms, the more recently created commercial banks in continental centres — though not in London — came to lend a hand to ensure the success of the operation. The system of underwriting new issues, though not altogether unknown in earlier centuries, developed during the 19th century and reached a very advanced stage, making for a higher degree of stability in the capital markets. Before the existence of underwriting syndicates in the modern sense, terms of bond issues had to be fixed in such a way as to allow a very wide safety margin so as to ensure that the public took up the entire amount. During the 18th century several British lottery loans were issued by the Government on such generous terms that they opened with premiums of up to 12 per cent. By the close of the 19th century it became possible to cut margins much finer, thanks largely to the development of the system of underwriting.

The development of modern money markets, especially in London, provided great assistance to the market for capital issues. Issuing houses and underwriters were able to raise short-term funds to tide them over temporary difficulties in placing the loans with the public.

A financial Press which was virtually non-existent in earlier centuries developed in the principal capital markets during the early 19th century. Although there was no lack of outspoken comment, the general attitude of financial commentators during the period preceding the first World War had not adequately conformed to the requirements of a well-informed financial Press, independent and fearless in its new service and in its comments. Indeed, right up to the early inter-war period the financial Press in general was much too timid and subservient when dealing with banks of importance. However, during the 'twenties and 'thirties gradually a more independent spirit came to prevail.

Before the first World War there was adequate, and at times more than adequate, competition between rival financial houses engaged in loan operations. Nevertheless, from time to time in certain sections of the market a leading bank or a group of banks succeeded in achieving a quasi-monipolistic position.

By and large, borrowers had succeeded in securing for themselves the terms that they deserved through their past record as debtors, their position at the time of the issue and their prospects. Between the wars, during the 'twenties, the pendulum swung in the opposite direction, in that cut-throat competition developed between rival financial centres as well as between rival firms in the same centres — though London issuing houses had upheld their tradition of abstaining from poaching on each other's preserves. Excessive competition among issuing houses caused unwarranted reductions of long-term interest rates on loans to borrowers with dubious prospects. As I pointed out in the last chapter, borrowers in Central Europe in particular were allowed to raise capital in amounts and on terms which had failed to allow for the extent of the risk involved.

Investors had absolute confidence in the stability of currencies in which loans were issued before the first World War. Fluctuations of those currencies were negligible and there was no such thing as exchange control. Devaluation scares and revaluation scares, too, were non-existent. The currency chaos resulting from the first World War came to an end during the 'twenties, and after the restoration of monetary stability the investing public came to trust the principal currencies once more. Although the dollar was easily the hardest amongst them, and the French franc after its stabilisation became harder than sterling during the late 'twenties, there was no difficulty whatsoever for London issuing houses to issue foreign loans in terms of sterling.

Before the first World War the process of long-term lending conformed to a high degree to the requirements of general economic stability. Broadly speaking, surplus countries were lending to deficit countries the surpluses available for that purpose, and highly developed countries were lending to developing countries. Things were not nearly so satisfactory between the wars. By that time Germany became a heavy borrower of capital in order to replace the capital wiped out by inflation. Until the late 'twenties France had more than enough domestic economic troubles and these, together with the heavy losses inflicted on French investors by defaults and repudiations of foreign loans, left them reluctant to resume lending abroad. Britain had to struggle with chronic unemployment resulting from the overvaluation of sterling and from structural economic changes. She was overlending from time to time and had to re-borrow abroad the resulting deficit on capital account. The largest lender, the United States, was in the throes of an unprecedented domestic boom which was fated to come to a bad end, even though few people realised it until October 1929. So long as it lasted it attracted foreign capital to New York, which meant that capital was flowing 'uphill' — from deficit countries to a surplus country. The absence of ideal equilibrium did not, however, prevent the lending countries from operating successfully and on an extensive scale.

Before the first World War *pax Britannica* ensured the necessary degree of international political stability for the satisfactory working of international capital markets. During the first half of the inter-war period, too, the international political outlook was satisfactory, as another major war was considered most unlikely. By the time the prospects became troubled by the advent of the Nazi régime, capital issuing activity came to a standstill in any case everywhere, as a result of the crises and the prolonged depression in the 'thirties.

There was no lack of creditworthy borrowers before the first World War. Although defaults by debtors were not infrequent, many countries honoured their financial undertakings very scrupulously and were always welcome whenever they wanted to raise more capital. All loans did not serve constructive purposes, however. France in particular was inclined to lend too much to her political allies to assist in financing their military preparations. As a result of the revolution in Russia and of political and financial difficulties in Eastern Europe, a very high proportion of pre-1914 loans came to be defaulted upon. Nevertheless, by the middle 'twenties lending centres were once more willing to lend and there were more than enough borrowers that were looked upon as creditworthy. Many of the defaulting debtors came to terms with their creditors and were able to resume borrowing abroad.

The level of long-term interest rates before 1914 was low. Although it rose considerably as a result of the first World War, it gradually declined during the 'twenties. Differentials in interest charges to various borrowers did not always express reasonably their relative creditworthiness, but broadly speaking all good borrowers were able to raise capital on tolerable terms. There were ample Stock Exchange facilities in the principal financial markets and also in the smaller centres for dealing in bonds subsequent to their issue.

Bans on issues were unknown before 1914, but Britain felt impelled to introduce between the wars a system of unofficial co-ordination of new issues which became formalised later with the establishment of the Capital Issues Committee.

Before the first World War there was very little official borrowing in the capital market by the authorities in the lending countries, except for the purpose of re-financing. Between the wars, too, until the Wall Street slump most of the market's capital resources were available for private requirements. During the long depression there was considerable Government borrowing for the purpose of financing public works to create employment, especially in the United States, and in the late 'thirties there was much new borrowing for rearmament. But during the 'thirties private demand for capital by eligible borrowers was in any case at a low ebb.

Taxes on new issues and transfers were very low everywhere until the post-war period. They certainly did not discourage issuing activities. Before 1914 direct taxation on interest income was very low. It rose considerably after the first World War, but even then it had not reached a level that would have discouraged issuing activities.

Throughout the 19th century and even more during the inter-war period monetary policy measures that had to be adopted for various reasons did handicap capital issuing activity from time to time, especially in London where the Bank of England pursued the traditions of widely fluctuating Bank rate. The Paris capital market was at an advantage because Bank rate changes were infrequent. In London whenever the Bank rate was raised to a high level, capital issuing activity in general and the issue of foreign loans in particular were temporarily discouraged. By and large, however, neither this nor the Stock Exchange fluctuations caused by the British monetary policy measures acted as a deterrent to capital issuing activities.

Let us now examine the extent to which the special requirements of a good market for foreign loans prevailed before the second World War. As already observed earlier in this chapter, the lending countries had by and large favourable balances of payments before 1914. Apart from a few isolated bad years,

Britain had a substantial perennial export surplus — allowing of course for invisible exports — and so had France and Germany. Britain's surplus declined after the first World War, while the French surplus on current account was more than wiped out by the flight of French capital. After the stabilisation of the franc at an undervalued level, the current export surplus was reinforced by repatriation of French capital, and ample resources became available for lending abroad. But owing to the heavy losses suffered by French investors on their pre-1914 foreign bonds, foreign issuing activity in Paris was well below the surplus available for that purpose. As for the United States her export surpluses during the inter-war period were inclined to be embarrassingly large. In addition there was a flow of capital to Wall Street during the 'twenties. American foreign lending was indeed on a large scale throughout the 'twenties, but a large part of it was thus re-borrowed.

Until the series of crises initiated by the Wall Street slump lenders and borrowers had no cause to fear revaluation or devaluation of the currencies in terms of which the foreign loans were issued. Loans in terms of sterling, dollars or other hard currencies were equally acceptable to all parties. Nevertheless, American issuing houses sought to safeguard the investors' interests by inserting a gold clause in the loan contracts. That clause was declared invalid by an Act passed in 1933.

There were no priorities for domestic borrowing which would have interfered with foreign issuing activities. We already saw that after the return to the gold standard Britain introduced, however, an unofficial embargo on foreign loans. During the 'thirties that embargo came to be reinforced and regularised, and was eventually made statutory. In practice foreign borrowers actually enjoyed priority in the London market before the second World War, because most issuing houses confined their activities to foreign loans and barely touched domestic capital issues.

Exchange restrictions were unknown during the years before 1914 and even during the inter-war period they barely affected the lending centres. On the other hand, restrictions operating in potential borrowing countries in the 'thirties tended to discourage long-term lending. All lending centres had good foreign exchange markets for the requirements of borrowers. There were also excellent short-term investment facilities in London and New York, in which borrowers were able to employ temporarily the unspent parts of their loans.

Although conditions in capital markets for the issue of foreign loans were not so favourable during the inter-war period as they had been before 1914, they were on the whole adequate and, until the advent of the crisis of the 'thirties, quite satisfactory. That crisis inflicted heavy losses on creditors, many of whom had already suffered losses in consequence of the first World War and its aftermath. The need for defending the currencies of lending countries, the advent of exchange control, and economic nationalism during the 'thirties between them drastically curtailed capital issuing activity. Such were the changes for the worse that it was indeed surprising that some of that activity revived at all in the late 'thirties, even if it was a bare fraction of the volume it had attained before 1914 and during the foreign issue boom of the 'twenties. The crisis of the 'thirties led to a widespread abandonment of the liberal policies towards foreign lending that had developed during the stable conditions of the 19th century. The outbreak of the second World War brought issuing activity for private purposes virtually to a standstill. All foreign lending came to assume the form of inter-Government transactions.

CHAPTER 4

POST-WAR MARKETS IN FOREIGN ISSUES

INTERNATIONAL capital markets were very slow in recovering from the effects of the crises of the 'thirties and of their virtually complete suspension during the second World War. For a long time during the post-war period general conditions did not favour a resumption of their activities, even though two of the markets, New York and Zurich, emerged from the war more or less unimpaired. In London, balance of payments conditions, exchange controls, currency uncertainties and political uncertainties resulting from the cold war tended to discourage for a long time a resumption of foreign issues. But in any case, a resumption of foreign issues would have received scant encouragement under the Labour Government, even if conditions had been favourable to it. The Chancellor of the Exchequer, Dr. Dalton, was openly hostile to international financial activities on ideological grounds. His attitude and that of his Government was characterised by a reply when pressed in Parliament to do something about the suspension of payments on the Japanese debt to British investors, to the effect that it served the British bondholders right to lose their money — why did they lend to Japan?

Capital resources available for foreign loans were curtailed during the post-war period partly by the effect of creeping inflation and partly by post-war equalitarianism as a result of which a smaller proportion of incomes tended to be saved. Moreover, in accordance with the spirit of the times, a larger proportion of corporation earnings was ploughed back into the firms instead of being made available to shareholders for reinvestment. On the other hand, capital requirements of the public sector of the economy greatly increased as a result of large Budgetary deficits through increased public spending on capital projects and the requirements of nationalised industries.

33

There were, moreover, abnormal domestic capital requirements of the private sector arising from physical reconstruction of war damage, re-equipment of plant worn out during the war, replenishment of greatly depleted supplies of every kind and the expansionary post-war economic policy in general.

Investors' willingness to acquire and hold fixed interest bearing securities in general and foreign bonds in particular was affected unfavourably by creeping inflation. It is true, the volume of outstanding foreign long-term indebtedness which was grossly excessive before the war declined in the meantime to more normal proportions, partly through gradual repayments in the absence of new borrowings and partly through a fall in the value of the currencies of the loan contracts. The same amount of foreign debt represented only about one-third of its pre-war burden in real terms, so that there was ample scope for a re-expansion of its total. Nevertheless, because past losses on foreign bonds were still remembered, owing to the post-war liquidity-preference of investors, and, above all, owing to the perennial inflationary trend, it became necessary to offer them high yields, apart from other reasons, in order to compensate them for the erosion of the purchasing power of their investment. The tendency in capital markets was distinctly in favour of equities and the yield on good-class equities declined well below that of Government loans.

London finance houses came to take an increased interest in domestic industrial capital issues. They all but lost interest in foreign loans for lack of opportunity. The same trend prevailed, though to a less pronounced extent, during the early post-war years in New York and other capital markets. However, as soon as opportunity for making foreign issues reappeared, issuing houses were able to resume where they left off some thirty years earlier. Generally speaking, issuing houses throughout the world have become in the meantime even more confidence-inspiring than they had been before the war, having weathered the banking crises of the 'thirties and having in many instances strengthened their position through amalgamations. Moreover, they increased their capital resources through becoming limited companies and attracting funds from the public instead of relying entirely on the family fortunes of their owners. Underwriting facilities have also improved because there are now many more institutional investors qualified to participate. The improvement of the machinery for foreign issues varied from country to country according to the degree of expansion of insurance companies, investment trusts, etc., and the degree of their freedom and willingness to invest in foreign loans.

Cut-throat competition that characterised the market for foreign issues during the 'twenties is no longer in evidence, but there is a sufficient degree of healthy competition to ensure fair terms for borrowers and to prevent an undue widening of the margin between what they pay and what the investors receive. Those margins vary widely according to capital market, largely owing to the differences in taxes.

Amidst the conditions of easy money that prevailed most of the time in lending countries during the post-war period, credits for temporary financing of foreign loan operations were most of the time easily obtainable. In more recent years the development of the Euro-currency markets has added considerably to such facilities in European capital markets, and so has the creation of the inter-bank money market in London. But chronic conditions of dear money in London and some other markets have added to the cost of financing foreign bond issues.

In respect of the outlook for currencies of the loan contracts the situation is incomparably less satisfactory than it had been before 1914, indeed even less satisfactory than during the 'twenties. From time to time investors came to suspect the currencies of the leading centres of a possible devaluation, or they come to be suspected by borrowers of a possible revaluation. The pre-war formula for protection against both through the insertion of a gold clause in the loan contract — which in any case had been applied almost exclusively to dollar loans — came to be discredited through the repudiation of the gold clause by the United States. In many countries the insertion of such a clause has been made unlawful.

While before the war economic instability through deflation was the danger, during the post-war period it was replaced by uncertainty caused by economic instability through inflation. From time to time measures against inflation in the lending countries came to handicap issuing activities. All the time many potential borrowers are under a cloud, owing to the acceleration of the pace of their domestic inflation. Political uncertainties, too, are now much more in evidence than during the 'twenties. It is true that at the time of writing acute fears of a third World War appear to have receded into the background. On the other hand, the possibility of the advent of Left-wing régimes in borrowing countries is now much more perturbing to investors. There is also from time to time the possibility of interference with foreign lending activity through the advent of Governments which are hostile to such activities.

Largely as a result of creeping inflation and of periodical repeated currency scares, long-term interest rates in the London capital market have been rather high. In Paris there is still a virtually complete ban on the issue of foreign securities, but in any case, owing to the level of interest rates prevailing there, the question does not arise. In Germany, in spite of the fact that savings are plentiful, a very large proportion of the available capital is mopped up by mortgage loans to finance building and construction. Interest rates in New York, Amsterdam and Zurich have been relatively low, but the extent to which it has been possible to take advantage of this in the last two markets has been kept down by official limitations on foreign issues.

Stock Exchange facilities are reasonably adequate in all post-war capital issue markets. Additional facilities have been provided by the development of the use of the Luxembourg Stock Exchange, in which listing new issues and dealing in bonds is free of tax.

There is now too much control of various kinds over issuing activity in most capital markets. Almost everywhere very elaborate steps have to be taken to obtain permission for foreign capital issues. In most markets *de jure* or *de facto* priorities are in operation.

Germany is the only European country in which the issue of foreign securities is completely free of any restrictions. In fact such issues actually enjoy a fiscal concession not extended to domestic issues. Germany has an embarrassingly large export surplus available for lending. But owing to the prevailing high long-term interest rates and issuing costs and also to the borrowers' fears that the D. mark might be revalued, the extent to which this freedom leads to actual foreign long-term borrowing is not proportionate to that of the facilities available. At the other extreme the issue of foreign securities is subject to an almost complete ban in France and up to the time of writing only loans in favour of countries of the Franc Area and of international institutions have been authorised. In Britain the ban on new issues is not so watertight. Exceptions have been made in favour of loans to the Sterling Area and to the EFTA countries, also in favour of refunding loans and loans whose proceeds are spent in Britain. Above all, the issue of foreign loans, whether in terms of sterling or of other currencies, is free if subscriptions are limited to non-residents or to residents paying with investment dollars. Although licences have to be applied for, this is little more than a formality.

In Belgium the authorisation of the Finance Ministry is required for foreign issues and such authorisation is liable to be refused for a variety of reasons. If authorised, resident subscribers have to pay with special investment currencies. The same rule applies in Holland where the foreign issues are permitted up to a maximum annual total and subject to limitations of the amount of individual transactions. In Switzerland the attitude of the authorities change according to balance of payments and other considerations. No foreign issues are permitted in Italy, except for international institutions.

There is now far too much official borrowing in most capital markets. In London in particular Government borrowing takes up a very high proportion of the available capital resources. Deficit financing by means of borrowing has become the accepted permanent state of affairs under the excuse that the money is needed for more or less 'productive' public capital expenditure. The Capital Issues Committee continues in Britain to function in respect of foreign issues.

Taxes imposed on new issues and on transfers of securities

are considerably higher than before the war. In Britain the stamp duty on new issues of bearer bonds is 2 per cent, in Belgium 1·6 per cent, in Italy it varies according to the nominal amount of the bonds. In France and Luxembourg there is no duty. In Germany there is a 2½ per cent tax. The duty on transfers of bonds was reduced in Britain in 1963 from 2 to 1 per cent, in Belgium it is 0·24 per cent, in France 0·6 per cent for spot transactions and 0·3 per cent for forward transactions. In Italy there is a ½ per cent annual tax on bonds in circulation and a nominal transfer duty. This list indicates the existence of wide discrepancies between the taxation on foreign bonds. In almost every instance the taxes are higher than before the war, but they are far from being prohibitive. Other costs associated with capital issues have also been increased though not disproportionately compared with the general trend of money values. They are much higher in London than in New York and much higher on the Continent than in London.

Taxation of investment incomes and of capital gains has increased considerably everywhere. The latter has been introduced in countries where it did not exist before the war. It tends to discourage taking risks, owing to the inadequacy of reward in the form of taxed yield and of capital profits. But in this respect, too, the situation is not intolerable.

Post-war monetary policy, especially in Britain, interfered from time to time with issuing activity in general to a much larger extent than in the old days, because, in addition to having to iron out boom and slump, it also has to protect the exchange and the gold reserve. This affects foreign bond issues particularly. The balance of payments position changed against foreign lending in London and during the 'sixties also against unrestricted lending in New York. The two main pre-war long-term lenders, Britain and the United States, are now burdened with a very large amount of foreign short-term indebtedness. This reduces their pre-war capacity of over-lending because, amidst the changed currency situation, it involves considerable risks. The rôle played by the pound and the dollar as reserve currencies has greatly curtailed the freedom of the two countries to issue foreign loans. The countries which, at the time of writing seem to be in the best position to lend abroad owing to their export surpluses, France and Germany, are unwilling or unable to do so on a sufficient scale.

Devaluation and revaluation fears affect facilities for foreign loans to a much larger extent than those for domestic capital issues. In respect of the latter, borrowers and lenders have the same currency, so that the problem does not present itself in such an acute form as in the case of foreign loans where one of the parties has to take an exchange risk.

Foreign exchange markets for the use by foreign borrowers are satisfactory. There are now ample short-term investment facilities at the disposal of foreign borrowers to employ their unspent balances profitably. The Euro-currency markets are used very extensively for that purpose.

From the above survey it is clear that, on balance, the conditions required for the issue of foreign loans are now not nearly as adequate as before the war. The markets which have adequate export surpluses at their disposal are either institutionally handicapped from lending those surpluses or they are subject to restrictions, while the markets which would be able and willing to do so are handicapped by the absence of a lendable export surplus. Exchange restrictions and restrictions on issuing activities interfere with the freedom of capital markets. Demand for capital runs high and exceeds supply, hence high interest rates. The prospects of a gradual depreciation of the monetary unit of the loans and the competition of equities offering a hedge against that depreciation as well as a possibility of capital gains, contribute towards maintaining interest rates on loans at a high level. In most countries taxation is high both on security issues and transfers and on the yield of the securities.

For a long time New York carried the burden of satisfying the high post-war demand for capital. London, although well equipped for lending abroad, was prevented from doing so by Britain's unsatisfactory balance of payments position. The extent to which Continental markets were able to participate is relatively limited. Nor has there been a satisfactory progress towards the integration of the capital markets of the European

Economic Community. Neither Paris nor Frankfurt has taken any distinct lead as a lending centre. The conclusion which emerges from these facts is that, in order to provide an alternative market to New York, an integration of the capital issuing activities of London and of the Continental lending centres is essential.

CHAPTER 5

ENTREPÔT FOR INTERNATIONAL CAPITAL

The rule that a country's ability to lend its domestic savings to foreign borrowers depends on the existence of an export surplus does not necessarily mean that countries without an export surplus during a given period are thereby absolutely precluded from lending to foreign borrowers during that particular period. A country which is in a strong financial position may be prepared to lend abroad on the assumption that in the following year it would have a surplus, and that by lending abroad it would actually assist towards the achievement of a surplus. Or it may be able to lend money borrowed from abroad, or to re-borrow money lent in excess of its export surplus, without subjecting its balance of payments to any strain. There is a strong case for performing such functions if the financial centre concerned possesses banks which inspire confidence abroad and have good international connections in addition to having an efficient mechanism enabling them to handle such transactions.

We saw in the last chapter that the capacity of all markets for the issue of foreign loans has declined in most respects more or less, compared with the active period between the wars and with the pre-1914 period. Even New York came to be affected by balance of payments difficulties during the late 'fifties and the early 'sixties. The United States authorities became very anxious by 1963 to divert from New York some of the foreign long-term borrowing and to encourage European markets to relieve New York of a large part of the burden which the dollar could no longer carry. But since each European market was in some ways handicapped and could not replace New York to any great extent, it became necessary for them to combine somehow their facilities in order to be able to relieve the dollar of the pressure due to overlending.

41

Had Britain joined the Common Market the integration of London's facilities for foreign capital issues with those of the other European financial centres would have been widely recognised as the obvious answer to the problem. As it is, the European centres concerned had to learn by experience that they were unable to take up the loans that New York was anxious to divert, without London's active participation, indeed without London's lead. But it was equally obvious that Britain was not in a position to replace the United States as a provider of capital on a large scale for foreign borrowers. Her balance of payments position was even worse than that of the United States. It is true, her annual deficits were not so intractable as those of the United States during the late 'fifties and early 'sixties, and the amounts involved were much smaller. But the United States was in an incomparably stronger technical position to stand the strain, in possession of a large if declining gold reserve. In spite of her heavy losses of gold, she could afford to lose more, even though it was becoming increasingly obvious that the drain could not continue indefinitely. For Britain even a relatively moderate aggravation of her gold drain as a result of overlending might have meant an acute crisis with a 7 per cent Bank rate to correct it.

A solution had to be found enabling London to resume its international banking function in the sphere of long-term lending without thereby aggravating the pressure on sterling. The solution lay in the adoption of the rôle of an entrepôt for foreign capital — that is, in lending to foreign borrowers, capital owned by non-resident investors.

Addressing the annual dinner given by the Lord Mayor of London to bankers and merchants of the City of London on October 3, 1962, the Governor of the Bank of England, Lord Cromer, declared: 'The time has now come when the City once again might well provide an international capital market where the foreigner cannot only borrow long-term capital but where ... he will once again wish to place his long-term placement capital. This entrepôt business in capital ... would not only fill a vital and vacant rôle in Europe in mobilising foreign capital for world economic development. It would be to the advantage of British industry in financing our customers.'

Lord Cromer's remark did not indicate the method by which
London should, in his opinion, fulfil the rôle of entrepôt of
capital. In a sense London, like practically every other
international financial centre, has always fulfilled that rôle to a
large extent. It has acted as an entrepôt mostly by re-lending to
foreign borrowers foreign deposits and other foreign funds held
in the form of short-term investments, but also by re-lending
foreign long-term capital invested in Britain in the form of
holdings of British securities and in other forms of long-term
investment.

A strong financial centre attracts foreign funds. Unless the
equivalent of these funds is kept in the form of additional gold
or official foreign exchange reserves, or is spent on additional
imports, it automatically assumes the form of an increase in the
short-term claims of the country concerned against other countries. Conversely, if a country overlends, unless the excess is
paid for in the form of gold export or a reduction of the official
reserve, or through a curtailment of imports or increase of
exports, it is automatically re-borrowed through a corresponding increase of the country's foreign short-term liabilities.

In any active international financial centre there are constant
flows of foreign capital in both directions, inward as well as
outward. To the extent to which the amounts lent abroad and
borrowed abroad are balanced the financial centre does fulfil
the rôle of entrepôt for foreign capital. This does not necessarily
mean that the individual institutions engaged in that transaction actually fulfil that part. Any one bank may be concerned
only with lending abroad or only with borrowing abroad. What
matters is that the financial centre or the country as a whole
re-lends the amount borrowed or re-borrows the amount lent.
In many instances the same banks both lend and borrow abroad,
but they need not borrow abroad for the purpose of lending
abroad. It just happens to work out that way.

London has long enjoyed the confidence of foreign countries
and many foreign investors have long been in the habit of
holding substantial amounts of securities in addition to holding
sterling deposits and short-term investments. London re-lent

these amounts — or, to be exact, amounts corresponding to those received, to foreign borrowers. Germany between the wars pursued the practice of borrowing abroad on short-term for the purpose of re-lending to Soviet Russia and other countries on long-term. In doing so she too performed the functions of an entrepôt for foreign capital. That rôle was performed even more distinctly by New York before the war. A very high proportion of dollar bonds issued there during the 'twenties found their way back to the borrowing countries or to other foreign countries. Moreover, citizens and institutions of countries borrowing from the United States invested in American securities or lent to Wall Street. What happened was that the United States re-borrowed part of the amounts lent abroad. This is what happened also in more recent times.

The Latin American countries, while borrowing abroad, also exported capital in the form of refugee funds owned by their citizens. The Soviet Union, too, is an active entrepôt of capital, having secured Government-guaranteed long-term credits of £100 million from Britain and promptly re-lending to Egypt an identical amount.

What Lord Cromer had in mind was something quite different from any of these practices. He envisaged the issue of foreign loans in London without the participation of British capital even in the form of re-lending borrowed foreign capital in such transactions. There is no question of re-borrowing or re-lending of foreign capital. London bankers are neither lenders nor borrowers, their function is confined to placing foreign bonds with foreign investors.

It is true, the London issuing houses and the underwriters may finance the transactions temporarily, pending the definite placing of the bonds with investors abroad. It is also true that British investors in foreign securities are also in a position to acquire the newly issued foreign bonds if they realise their investments in order to secure the investment dollars required, or if they acquire such investment dollars from other former British holders of foreign securities. But in substance such transactions simply amount to turning over existing foreign investment. No additional British capital is lent abroad.

London is merely acting as intermediary between foreign borrowers and foreign investors, and the latter provide all the capital lent by London. Or, the foreign securities are acquired by U.K. residents from other U.K. residents.

Apart from the two exceptions mentioned above, British residents are not in a position to take up those bonds. For this reason the requirements of such a market for new issues differ materially in many respects both from those of a capital market for domestic borrowers and those of a capital market which lends local capital or borrowed foreign capital to foreign borrowers.

Most foreign loans issued in London during 1963–64 were issued in U.S. dollars, though a number of them were issued in composite units of account. One loan for Japan was issued in terms of sterling, but it was for repayment of a maturing debt. Some sterling loans were also made to countries of the Sterling Area or to EFTA countries. In some instances the issue was made in sterling denomination with D. marks as the alternative currencies, but such issues, too, were subject to restrictions. What is essential is not the currency of denomination but the condition that British residents are only entitled to subscribe or buy such bonds with the aid of investment dollars.

The issue of foreign bonds in foreign currency denominations does not necessarily mean that the issuing centre is confined to the rôle of an entrepôt for capital. We saw earlier that many international loans issued during the 'twenties in terms of sterling or dollars had tranches issued in Switzerland or Holland, which countries were quite willing to take up bonds in denominations of a foreign currency. In our days, too, residents in many countries are entitled to acquire and hold bonds in terms of a foreign currency. The issuing centre assumes the rôle of entrepôt, in the sense in which the term was employed by Lord Cromer, if residents do not acquire such loans in circumstances in which the transaction would entail a net export of capital, and the whole amount of the capital lent to foreign borrowers is contributed by non-residents. This does not necessarily mean that the amount lent is capital newly exported by foreign countries. Large parts of the subscribers may pay for the bonds with the aid of sterling held on non-resident account which the holders are of course entitled to invest wherever they like. This again does not entail an export of British capital. What happens is that sterling which is already in foreign hands is lent to other foreign residents.

The differences between the requirements of an international capital market in which local capital is lent and one which serves as an entrepôt for foreign capital may be summarised as follows:

(1) There is no need for such a capital market to possess plentiful supplies of local savings in excess of local requirements of capital.

(2) The attitude of local investors towards foreign investments is of no great importance.

(3) There is no need for the country in which the foreign loans are issued to have a balance of payment surplus.

(4) It is immaterial if the local currency is subject to devaluation or revaluation rumours, since it is not the currency in terms of which the loans are issued.

(5) The currency of the loan contract, on the other hand, should not be suspected of being likely to be revalued or devalued.

(6) Exchange restrictions affecting the local currency are a disadvantage, but unless they also affect transactions between non-residents they do not prevent foreign issuing activity.

(7) It is an advantage, though not of decisive importance, if the financial centre has a good market in Euro-dollars and other Euro-currencies.

(8) It is an advantage, though not of decisive importance, if local residents are in a position to subscribe with the aid of investment dollars or currencies of a similar type.

(9) The foreign bonds issued must be listed on Stock Exchanges both in the issuing centres and abroad.

(10) Above all, it is essential that the issuing banks should have good connections with banks and investors abroad.

Since loans in terms of foreign currencies are issued primarily for non-resident investors — apart from resident investors who want to switch their foreign investments or who replace other

U.K. investors — the supply of local capital is immaterial. Generally speaking, however, confidence in a financial centre presupposes adequacy of domestic financial resources. It is difficult to visualise a country that is a persistent net borrower abroad being able to fulfil adequately the rôle of an entrepôt for foreign capital. What matters more is that the countries in which the bonds are placed by the issuing houses of the entrepôt centre should possess adequate supplies of capital for that purpose.

For the above reason, the attitude of local investors is of no decisive importance. Nevertheless, since many of the large institutional investors in the country that issues the loans play the part of underwriters, their attitude is not a matter of indifference. Moreover, subscriptions with the aid of investment dollars may contribute marginally to the success of the issues.

As I said above, there is no need for a country acting as entrepôt for foreign capital to have a balance of payments surplus. On the other hand, a substantial perennial balance of payments deficit might undermine confidence in the financial centre concerned and this would be detrimental to the prestige of its banks and to its rôle as an entrepôt. Likewise, there is no need for the local currency to be absolutely above suspicion either in respect of the possibility of a devaluation or in that of a revaluation. If, however, there is an acute wave of distrust its psychological effect and its effect on the Stock Exchange might be detrimental to the ability of the financial centre to fulfil its task efficiently, if at all. Issuing houses and underwriters may be reluctant to assume new commitments, for fear of adverse Stock Exchange trends and difficult credit conditions. What matters more is that the currency of the contract should not be suspect. The loans have to be issued in a currency which at the time of the transaction is not suspected by borrowers of being likely to be revalued or by lenders of being likely to be devalued. The problem is to select a currency which is hard but not too hard. During the early 'sixties the dollar met that requirement to a very high degree.

The country in which the bonds are issued need not be

47

entirely free of exchange restrictions, but those in force must not apply to non-residents. Above all, the currency of the loan contract must not be restricted for non-residents. It is essential that they should be in a position to sell the proceeds of their investments at any time at current exchange rates. It is also important that they should be at liberty to employ their balances on non-resident account in the entrepôt centre for subscribing to or buying bonds issued in the market concerned.

We saw in the previous chapter that availability of short-term credit facilities is an essential condition of a good capital market. This applies equally to markets acting as entrepôt; they are in need of Euro-dollar and other Euro-currency facilities, or other forms of short-term credit, for the temporary financing of their bond issues.

Even though the rôle of entrepôt implies the placing of the foreign bonds abroad, it helps if issuing houses can depend on being able to place at least some of them locally. For this reason it is an advantage if the special exchange rate at which local residents are entitled to acquire currencies required for paying for foreign bonds is not at too heavy a discount against the ordinary exchange rate.

It is essential for the bonds to be listed not only on the Stock Exchange of the issuing centre but also on one or several Stock Exchanges abroad. It is a particular advantage if they can be listed on the Stock Exchange of the country in whose currency the bonds are issued, which is the reason why some European dollar bonds issues are listed in Wall Street, even if there is no present demand for them. But this is not an indispensable condition. It helps a great deal if the issuing houses have branches or affiliates in countries where they want to place the bonds. This is probably one of the reasons why several London banking houses have opened branches or affiliates abroad in recent years. The issuing houses must have good clients among investors abroad, especially among those possessing non-resident sterling or Euro-currency deposits in London.

The creation and maintenance of an entrepôt for foreign capital entails considerable advantages. The advantages to borrowers are obvious, especially if a situation arises in which a financial centre with ample experience and efficient technical organisation for foreign issues is prevented by its balance of payments position from lending its domestic capital or from re-lending borrowed capital, and if centres with ample resources available for lending do not possess the necessary technical organisation or are prevented from lending abroad by institutional inhibitions. From the point of view of the country acting as entrepôt the advantages are not confined to the invisible exports represented by the commissions earned on the transactions. As likely as not the proceeds of the loans may be employed by the borrowers for buying goods in the country of the entrepôt centre. The issuing houses are enabled to recover and maintain their technique which might become rusty if the balance of payments position of their country prevents them over a prolonged period from keeping up their practice by issuing loans taken up by local investors.

Above all, the possibility of acting as entrepôt for foreign capital enables the market playing that rôle to co-operate closely with markets possessing ample capital resources and a favourable balance of payments. This is essential from the point of view of achieving an integration in European capital markets. Kindleberger pointed out in an article appearing in the *Weltwirtsdaftliches Archiv* in 1963 that eight years after the conclusion of the Treaty of Rome there was no integration between the capital markets of the six EEC countries. Within a few months after this observation was published the reappearance of London as a lender, in spite of the fact that its rôle was confined to that of an entrepôt, has resulted in a remarkable progress towards the integration of the European capital markets, though France has continued to keep aloof from it.

CHAPTER 6

THE MARKET IN DOLLAR BONDS

ALTHOUGH the post-war practice of foreign long-term lending in the form of dollar bonds issued in Europe developed in Continental centres already during the late 'fifties, not until London came to take an active hand in 1963 did it come to assume really considerable proportions. On the Continental markets part of the foreign issuing activity assumed the form of bonds in terms of their respective local currencies. In particular, foreign loans were issued in Germany in terms of D. marks and in Switzerland in terms of Swiss francs. Although it was technically possible for London to issue foreign loans for non-residents in terms of sterling, the dollar was chosen in preference to sterling in all but the few instances mentioned in the last chapter — loans to the Sterling Area, to EFTA countries and for re-financing. There were only a few other foreign loans issued in terms of sterling which offered to subscribers the choice between sterling and D. marks. The rest of the foreign loans were issued either in terms of dollars or in terms of composite units of account, mostly the former.

We saw in Chapter 4 that since the war the ability of each of the Continental financial centres to issue foreign loans has been, for various reasons, limited, and that it would have been clearly beyond their resources to handle the entire volume of additional loans diverted from New York as a result of announcement of the Interest Equalisation Tax. It was, therefore, essential that London should participate once more in foreign capital issuing activity, even if British residents remained precluded by exchange restrictions from active participation in such loans. In fact during the twelve months that followed the announcement of the Interest Equalisation Tax London assumed the lead for the issue of foreign dollar bonds.

No data are available about London's participation in the

50

various loans which were issued partly in other countries. As
these loans are not offered to the public the respective amounts
of the participations of various members of the consortium did
not have to be published, though some prospectuses did volun-
teer that information. In any case, it was immaterial how
much of the total the London members of the consortium
handled, because even London's share was placed with investors
outside the United Kingdom. What mattered was that in the
majority of issues of dollar bonds in which London participated
some London issuing house headed the consortium. By
implication Continental banks accepted London's lead in these
international transactions. This in spite of the fact that the
British investors' rôle in taking up these dollar bonds was
necessarily very limited.

Theoretically it was possible for U.K. residents to subscribe
to such loans either through acquiring investment dollars in the
market or through switching their existing dollar investments.
In practice the high premium ruled out the subscriptions
through buying investment dollars. Conceivably in some situation it might have appeared convenient for British holders of
dollar securities to switch into newly issued dollar bonds, but the
volume of such operations could not have represented more than
a fraction of the issue. On the other hand, there is a fair scope
for investing in such bonds the reserves and pension funds of
British subsidiaries abroad. This is understood to have been
done in fact on a fairly considerable scale. Even so, it must
represent a minor part of the total dollar bonds issued through
London. The bulk of the capital raised here was bound to
come from non-resident accounts in London or from accounts
of foreign investors with banks in other countries.

London is one of the three main international centres for
refugee funds in the broadest sense of the term, the other two
being New York and Switzerland. London banks handle a
large number of accounts for non-residents who keep their funds
here for a variety of reasons. Funds on these accounts may
have the legal status of non-resident sterling, or they may be
Euro-dollar or other Euro-currency accounts. Holders of such
accounts may find it advantageous in given circumstances to

invest in European dollar bonds. Many foreign clients of British banks may subscribe with the aid of their funds on their accounts in foreign centres. Many British people who took up more or less permanent residence abroad are still in contact with their London banks. They are therefore potential investors in such dollar bonds. One of the most active London issuing houses claims to be able to place its dollar bond issues with some 150 foreign banks, institutional investors, and large private investors all over the world.

Even so, London banks would not be able to handle large amounts of dollar issues unless they were associated in the transaction with a number of Continental banks. On the published prospectus there is usually the name of one or more London issuing houses and also those of several Continental countries, amongst them in many instances those of the borrowing countries themselves. This latter fact indicates that a large proportion of these dollar loans is usually taken up by investors in the borrowing countries themselves. At first sight this might appear futile, since the foreign exchange position of their monetary authorities does not improve if the funds are provided by their own nationals who pay for the bonds in local currency. But the arrangement does provide a convenient formula under which the governments of the countries concerned can borrow from their own nationals in terms of dollars without loss of face for issuing a domestic loan in terms of a foreign currency. In certain instances the investor in the borrowing country trusts the borrower's solvency while distrusting their local currency. Or he may prefer bonds issued in a leading financial centre because they have a wider market than they are likely to have if issued locally.

If the composition of the consortium for issues of dollar bonds is international, that of the underwriting syndicate is even more so. It often includes banks in practically all Western European countries. London banks themselves participate in each other's issues on a basis of reciprocity. New York banks, too, participate occasionally in the European issues, even though their clients in the United States are prevented by the Interest Equalisation Tax from subscribing.

Some loans are placed firmly in advance of their formal issue, while others are unloaded by the issuing houses or underwriters gradually. None of the dollar loans that are issued in London are offered for subscription to the public, for the simple reason that, apart from the exceptions indicated above, U.K. residents are not in a position to apply. Continental issues, on the other hand, are usually available for the rank and file of local investors. Sub-underwriting is usually taken by many insurance companies, investment trusts, Stock Exchange firms, etc., who are prepared to retain for themselves or for their clients the bonds they have to take up or who definitely take over their bonds on sub-underwriting terms.

There is no restriction on the acquisition of dollar bonds by residents in Western Germany or in Switzerland. Indeed in Germany such issues are not subject to the 25 per cent tax on domestic issues acquired by foreign residents. French residents are in theory free to acquire foreign securities, but foreign issues are not authorised. In any case portfolio investments abroad are surrounded by measures of strict Government supervision of the kind that is disliked by French investors. In Holland and Belgium investors can only subscribe with the aid of investment currencies similar to British investment dollars, but since the premium on such investment currencies is kept down by official intervention to a very low figure in practice this is no obstacle to local subscription. Indeed the very existence of a remote possibility that the Dutch or Belgium authorities might discontinue their support of the respective investment currencies in their countries provides an inducement for the acquisition of dollar bonds and other foreign securities by local residents. For if, as a result of a suspension of the official support, the premium on investment currencies should widen, Dutch or Belgian holders of foreign securities would stand to benefit by it when they realise their holdings and the proceeds of their holdings.

Foreign funds on accounts with banks in Switzerland or elsewhere, especially accumulated Middle East oil royalties, are potential sources of investment in dollar bonds. So are refugee funds from every part of the world deposited in any financial centre. Once they are outside their countries of origin, exchange controls applied there cannot prevent their owners from acquiring dollar bonds. Since principal and interest can be made payable, at the bondholders option, in the United States or in any country in which the debtor has paying agents, the bonds are convenient investments for holders of refugee funds who trust the dollar.

Judging by the large number of such issues, the market for them must have a fairly substantial absorbing capacity. After each run of such issues it was widely suggested that 'saturation point' had now been reached. But before long further issues appeared and were easily absorbed by investors.

Borrowing countries for whose benefit such dollar bonds are issued include Japan, Denmark, Norway, Finland, Italy, Portugal, Austria, Belgium — which country is both borrower and lender — and Israel. Japan, Denmark and Italy have been so far the largest borrowers. The actual borrowers include Governments, Government-controlled industries, public utilities, municipal authorities, insurance companies and private industrial and commercial concerns. Such corporations often raise loans in the form of issuing convertible debentures.

The bonds are repayable mostly between ten and twenty years and their interest varies mostly between 5½ and 6½ per cent. They are usually issued slightly under par. They are not secured as a rule by any specific security, but in some instances they are Government-guaranteed, or the Central Bank concerned gives an undertaking to provide the exchange for the payment of interest and the repayment of principal. In this latter respect the terms vary considerably according to the views the issuing houses take about the need for safeguarding bondholders specifically against future exchange control measures.

Several Danish issues, for instance, contain a clause according to which the borrower will be permitted under Danish law and regulations *now in force*, to purchase the dollars required for the loan service. Evidently such a clause does not safeguard bondholders against a possible future reinforcement of exchange control. The issues for the Istituto per la Ricostruzione Industriale—a corporation owned by the Italian Government—contains a similarly inadequate clause which does not prevent the Government from blocking the transfer of interest and principal by simply changing the law. On the other hand, the prospectus of a Finnish issue contained a paragraph stating that the Bank of Finland has 'confirmed in writing that it will authorise before the due dates the free transfer of the U.S. dollars required for the service of the Bond Certificates'. A Portuguese Government loan contains an even more watertight provision: 'The Republic of Portugal undertakes to transfer or make available all funds required for the service of the Bonds . . . in U.S. dollars under all circumstances without any limitations and outside any bilateral or multilateral payments or clearing agreement to which the Republic of Portugal may be a party at the times these payments are made'.

Such a watertight formula should be applied to all loan contracts. Failing that it should be made plain that the Government of the borrowers reserve the right to suspend at any time the transfer of the dollars for the debt service. Investors who are prepared to take that risk should be enabled to do so with their eyes open. It is true, in the case of some countries, the risk of future exchange control is not nearly so grave as in the case of others. Even so, as the situation in that respect is liable to change suddenly, issuing houses should deem it their duty to secure for their clients the largest possible measure of safeguards.

Since none of the Governments concerned appear to have had any objection to safeguarding bondholders against deduction of taxes, *present or future*, there could be no logical reason for withholding similar safeguards in respect of future exchange control.

The payment of interest and principal is 'in U.S. dollars in the form of a transfer to a bank in the United States or of a dollar cheque paid in the United States, subject to the regulations in the country of the recipient'. This clause appears in practically every loan contract, and its only variation is for loans which are payable also in other currencies, for which similar provisions are inserted in respect of payment in those currencies.

The bonds are listed on the Stock Exchanges of the countries participating in the issue and also on the Luxembourg Stock Exchange. In some instances they are also listed on the New York Stock Exchange, in spite of the fact that the Interest Equalisation Tax reduces the chances of active dealings in them in the United States. But some issuing houses envisage the possibility that the Interest Equalisation Tax might be allowed to expire at the end of 1965, in which case, an active market might develop on Wall Street in the European dollar bonds.

Transactions in European dollar bonds are mostly outside Stock Exchanges. In this respect the position is somewhat similar to foreign dollar bonds that had been issued in New York, dealings in which are to a large extent not in Wall Street but over the counters of banks. The reason for this is that fluctuations in the prices on such bonds are very often too narrow to allow for sufficient profit margins to stand the cost of transactions through Stock Exchanges.

All the bonds are bearer bonds and are free of any with-holding tax. London is now able to issue such bonds, because the ban on bearer bonds adopted at the beginning of the war for the purposes of exchange control has been lifted. This has removed one of the main obstacles to a resumption of foreign loan issuing actively in the London market.

There is a certain amount of arbitrage between various centres. Firms specialising in such transactions take advantage of discrepancies between the various quotations of the same securities in different centres, also of discrepancies that are liable to develop between prices of bonds which are comparable with each other — for instance between Norwegian and Danish municipal issues.

The largest proportion of European dollar bonds is believed to have been placed in Switzerland, mostly not with Swiss investors but with foreign holders of accounts with Swiss banks. For this reason there is an active turnover in dollar bonds in Zurich. There is a fairly large turnover also in London, both on the Stock Exchange and over the counter. Members of the Stock Exchange have to offer them first to the market and can only sell them outside if they are unable to get the price asked for. The margins quoted by jobbers on the Stock Exchange are often wider than those obtainable from merchant banks and other firms specialising in such transactions. These latter margins are at times so narrow that they do not allow for brokers' commissions, which is one of the reasons why so much of this business bypasses the Stock Exchange in spite of some obvious advantages of dealing on the Stock Exchange.

Transactions in dollar bonds are rather complicated, since often they have to be delivered abroad. Arbitrage in them is a highly specialised branch of activity, involving a thorough knowledge of the conditions in which such business is transacted abroad, such as delivery terms, taxation, exchange control, etc. While until some years ago the number of firms engaged in such arbitrage was small, and margins were wide, the increase in their number has resulted in a narrowing of margins.

A question which is often asked but is seldom answered is about the absorbing capacity of the European market in dollar bonds. With such bond issues coming out in frequent intervals during 1963–64 everybody concerned was wondering when saturation point would be reached. As we saw above, in only a few Continental countries are investors free to subscribe to foreign bonds. Germany is by far the most important amongst them, but since the D. mark appears to be harder than the dollar, German investors are not particularly attracted by dollar bonds. In any case quite a number of foreign D. mark loans were issued in Germany in 1964.

Nevertheless, the markets seemed to have had no difficulty in absorbing a large number of dollar loans. In examining the question of its absorbing capacity we must distinguish between the absorbing capacity of issuing houses and underwriters and that of the ultimate investors. As it usually takes time to place the bonds, the financial mechanism engaged in the task is apt to become clogged from time to time with undigested issues. What matters is that they should be unloaded in the course of time, making room for the next issue. Once the absorbing capacity of the investing public itself has become exhausted, issuing activity must come to a halt until new capital becomes available. Natural accumulation of savings replace the funds invested but, once most investors interested in that type of investment had acquired all they wanted, an increase of their available resources which would enable them to acquire more dollar bonds is bound to be a gradual and slow process.

A substantial increase in the absorbing capacity of the market for dollar bonds may occur through the following causes:

(1) Additional refugee funds may become available. For instance, the flight of Italian capital to Switzerland in 1963–64 provided additional funds for investment in dollar bonds.

(2) The dollar may become more attractive to investors, through becoming harder because of an improvement in the balance of payments of the United States, the adoption of a disinflationary policy, etc.

(3) Government measures may divert capital from alternative investment. For instance, the imposition of a 25 per cent Capital Yield Tax in Germany on securities held by non-residents must have induced some holders to switch into dollar bonds.

(4) Relaxation of exchange control measures in the issuing countries or in the investing countries.

(5) Decline in the premium on investment dollars and other similar currencies

(6) Relaxation of inhibitions which prevent institutional investors from investing in such types of securities.

On the other hand, the absorbing capacity of the market is liable to contract for the following reasons:

(1) Repatriation of refugee funds. For instance, French funds returned to France after the consolidation of conditions there under de Gaulle.

(2) Confidence in the dollar might weaken.

(3) Government measures diverting capital from New York to the market for European dollar bonds might become mitigated or reversed. For instance the Interest Equalisation Tax might not be renewed in its original form when it expires at the end of 1965.

(4) Exchange control measures might be reinforced.

(5) The premium on investment dollars and similar currencies might increase.

The above list is by no means exhaustive and there is an ever-present possibility of unexpected changes in the absorbing capacity of the market. As far as issuing houses and underwriters are concerned, their absorbing capacity, too, is open to changes, but ultimately it depends on that of the investors.

CHAPTER 7

INTERNATIONAL INTEREST RATES

My book on Euro-dollars describes and analyses the system of international short-term interest rates that has come into being through the development of the Euro-dollar market. This set of interest rates is distinct from, and to a large measure independent of, domestic short-term interest rates prevailing either in New York or in the European financial centres where the transactions in Euro-dollars take place. An expansion of the European market for dollar bonds would apply this system to long-term interest rates. At the time of writing the issues of such bonds are not on a sufficiently large scale and the turnover in existing bonds is not nearly sufficiently active or continuous to justify a contention that such a level of international long-term interest rates is already actually in existence. Should the issues become frequent and/or larger, and should the turnover in the bonds after their issue expand considerably, a distinct structure of interest rates and yields would emerge which might operate in the sphere of long-term loans in some ways similar to the operation of international short-term interest rates in the Euro-dollar market.

Even on the basis of the present volume of activity in the European dollar bond market it is possible to discern, in theory if not in practice, a set of international interest rates whose level is distinct from that of the New York foreign bond market on the one hand and those of the foreign bond markets in London and other Western European capital issue markets on the other. It is, of course, more difficult to ascertain standard rates in bond markets than in Euro-currency markets. In the latter the rates quoted at any given moment to first-rate banks of a financially strong country which has not been over-borrowing, are fairly uniform, even though European branches of American banks pay slightly lower rates, because they are always expected to be in a position to deliver dollars as a matter of course, while it is possible to envisage situations in which exchange restrictions might prevent even first-rate non-American banks from repaying Euro-dollar deposits. In bond markets interest rates vary much more widely, depending as they do on the standing of the borrower and on the security of the loan and on other of its terms. Nevertheless, it might be possible to single out the rates paid by the best class of borrowing Governments as the representative rate for the market.

The interest rate on dollar bonds for first-rate borrowers — such as, for instance, Scandinavian Governments — was during 1964 around 5½ per cent. The actual yield is slightly higher. This is distinctly above the yield on bonds of a corresponding class in New York, Zurich and Amsterdam, but it is distinctly lower than corresponding bond yields in London, Frankfurt or Paris. Relatively speaking, the yield on good-class dollar bonds is only moderately higher than interest rates on long-term Euro-dollar deposits. The relatively narrowness of the differential can be explained on the ground of a vague anticipation of a decline in interest rates over long periods, or on the ground that time deposits have to be held until maturity while bonds can be sold at any time, even though their holders run the risk of having to sell at a loss if they need the cash urgently.

This structure of long-term international interest rates, such as it is, is of course not altogether independent either of the domestic interest rate structure of the United States or of the countries where the bonds are issued or acquired, any more than Euro-dollar rates are independent of short-term rates in New York, London and other money centres. It is undoubtedly affected to a large extent by conditions outside the United States. It may be said to have a separate existence from that of long-term interest rates in the United States. Most of these dollar bonds are not quoted on Wall Street, and in any case, in view of the effect of the Interest Equalisation Tax, the bonds have at present no attraction for law-abiding U.S. residents. For this reason, the interest differentials in favour of European dollar bonds would have to widen very considerably before it

61

would give rise to a sufficient demand by U.S. residents to result in an adjustment in New York quotations of European bonds that had been issued in the United States prior to the announcement of the new tax.

Nevertheless, these bonds do compete for American residents' funds which sought refuge abroad for fiscal reasons or in anticipation of future exchange restrictions in the United States. They also compete to some extent for funds owned legitimately by Americans resident abroad or by foreign subsidiaries of American firms. Decisions by holders of such funds whether or not to invest in European dollar bonds in preference to bonds issued in New York are not influenced, however, entirely by interest differentials.

Broadly speaking, the level, trend and fluctuations of international long-term interest rates is influenced (*a*) by interest rate factors, (*b*) by Stock Exchange factors, and (*c*) by foreign exchange factors. The actual factors affecting the issue terms and subsequent yields of European dollar bonds may be listed under the following headings:

(1) The amounts of foreign dollar bonds that are being issued or are outstanding in Europe.

(2) The degree of popularity of this type of investment among investors outside the United States.

(3) The level of local long-term interest rates in countries where the bonds are issued, and in countries where they are eventually placed.

(4) The degree of liquidity of the capital markets in which the bonds are issued or placed.

(5) The views taken by investors on the prospects of the dollar.

(6) The views taken by investors on the prospects of their own currency.

(7) Euro-dollar or other Euro-currency deposit rates and future prospects of such rates.

(8) Forward dollar rates and other relevant forward rates if the transactions are financed with the aid of other currencies and if the exchange risk is covered.

(9) The views taken by investors on the prospects of interest rates and bond yields in general.

(10) The level and trend of prices of comparable foreign bonds in Wall Street.

(11) Effectiveness of exchange control in preventing residents in the countries concerned from acquiring the bonds.

(12) The level of the premium on investment dollars or on similar currencies.

(13) The degree of international competition between banks for handling the new issues.

(14) The ability and willingness of issuing houses and under-writers to nurse a loan that was undersubscribed.

(15) Competition of alternative facilities available to bor-rowers for covering their capital requirements.

The volume of European dollar bonds available for investors depends on the volume of new issues of such bonds and the willingness of holders of European dollar bonds to sell their holdings. There has been so far no even flow of new issues which usually appear in batches with intervals of weeks or even months during which there are hardly any new issues. Nor is there any really regular flow of dealings in earlier issues on any of the Stock Exchanges or, for that matter, over the counter. Issuing houses and underwriters usually place privately their portions of the issues and those acquiring the bonds usually do so with the intention of holding them. Nevertheless, there is a certain amount of turnover in many of the bonds. The prices at which they change hands should convey some idea about the trend of interest rates and influence the terms of new bond issues.

The popularity of European dollar bonds among investors outside the United States depends partly on general considerations such as the interest investors take in acquiring bonds in general and foreign bonds in particular, confidence in the dollar, local and international political conditions in the lending country, etc. But it is also affected by the availability of, and yield on, alternate investment facilities. Foreign bonds quoted in Wall Street have the advantage of a much broader market and for this reason alone even for non-residents who are not affected by the Interest Equalisation Tax they are more attractive than European bonds, unless the latter offer a higher yield. Any change in the differentials is liable to affect the demand for European dollar bonds.

That demand is also affected by the level of local long-term rates in countries where they are issued. The extent of this influence depends largely on the extent to which local residents are permitted to subscribe. We saw earlier that in Germany and Switzerland there is no restriction on acquiring such bonds, and even in Holland and Belgium investors are in a position to do so with the aid of investment dollars which are at a nominal premium against the current exchange rate. As far as these countries are concerned, yields of the dollar bonds have to compete against those of comparable domestic bond issues. On the other hand, in countries such as Britain, where exchange control greatly reduces the possibility of subscriptions by residents, as far as these residents are concerned the bonds have only to compete against yields of foreign bonds which local residents are entitled to replace by the new bonds.

When the bonds are placed outside the countries in which they are issued then the interest rates in the countries where the issues are made matter naturally less than the interest rates in countries whose residents acquire the bonds. Even so, these bonds may be regarded by non-residents as alternative investments to the local bonds of countries in which they are issued. For instance, a Continental investor may acquire dollar bonds issued in London as an alternative to buying sterling bonds, domestic or foreign, with the aid of security sterling bought at a small discount.

We saw in the last chapter that, to a large extent, the dollar bonds are acquired by residents of the borrowing countries themselves if they have full confidence in the solvency of the borrower but wish to hold dollar securities because they may not altogether trust the stability of the local currency, or because they assume that dollar bonds have a better market. When the bonds are acquired as a hedge against a devaluation of the local currency the yield is a secondary consideration. The attraction of being able to rely on a good bond market may induce investors to be content with a lower yield for the sake of the prospects of obtaining a better price when realising the bonds.

Interest rates in the issuing countries determine the cost of the temporary financing of the issues until the bonds are placed with investors. On the assumption that this can be completed in a matter of days or weeks, interest charges for such a brief period should not materially affect the terms on which issuing houses and underwriters are prepared to handle the issue. But if they envisage the possibility of having to nurse a large part of the issue for months they have to consider the costs when negotiating the terms. Indeed the high cost of the temporary financing of the issues might even induce banks to decline participating in the transaction.

The cost of short-term financing of the transactions with the aid of borrowed Euro-currencies depends partly on the cost of covering the exchange risk. Unless it is deemed safe to leave that risk uncovered, forward rates are to some extent liable to influence the cost of short-term financing of the issues and the terms on which issuing houses and underwriters are willing to participate.

Apart altogether from the level of local short-term interest rates affecting the cost of financing the transactions, conditions of liquidity in the capital markets concerned are also liable to affect interest rates on bonds. General conditions of liquidity as well as the cost of short-term financing are apt to influence issuing houses and underwriters in their decision whether to assume new commitments.

Since there is no means of knowing how much of the participations in the issue have to be carried and for how long it has to be carried, financing is usually effected with the aid of money at call or at very short notice. That being so, the prospects of tighter conditions in the near future carry the possibility of having to renew these loans at a higher cost.

The volume of funds available for investing the dollar bonds is apt to change. Since these bonds are not everybody's cup of tea, the appearance of a number of issues in close succession might congest the market. We saw in the last chapter that the absorbing capacity of the market is liable to become reduced through various circumstances. When that happens, issuing houses and underwriters prefer to forgo the deal unless the terms are made attractive enough to induce the type of investor to whom these bonds appeal to realise other holdings of similar bonds for the sake of investing in the new issues and to induce new sets of investors to take an interest in them. Otherwise issuing houses might deem it necessary to wait with the next bond issue until more funds available for the purpose have been accumulated by the existing limited range of investors who are inclined to acquire them. Self-respecting borrowers are reluctant to consent to paying higher interest rates for fear of its detrimental effects on their prestige. For this reason among others, international long-term interest rates are much less flexible than international short-term interest rates.

An all-important consideration affecting the interest rates is the view taken about the prospects of the dollar. When there appears to be the slightest possibility of its devaluation it deters a high proportion of potential investors, while others are only interested if the yield compensates them for the additional risk. With the restoration of confidence in the dollar during 1963–64 the bonds have become distinctly more attractive on terms at which they would have been deemed unattractive during the years of recurrent acute dollar scares.

European dollar bonds are apt to be used extensively as a hedge against a devaluation of the investors' local currency. For this reason the views taken by residents in the countries concerned about the prospects of their own currencies are liable to influence demand for these bonds. Revaluation prospects of the investors' own currencies are also an important factor. Residents in West Germany or Switzerland are not likely to acquire long-term dollar bonds of any kind if they anticipate a revaluation of the D. mark or the Swiss franc, unless the yield compensates them for the risk involved. On the other hand, residents in a country whose currency is under a cloud might try to hedge against its devaluation by acquiring dollar bonds even at a relatively low yield — provided that they can do so under the exchange regulations, or that they can evade those regulations.

Borrowers on their part are not likely to concede a higher yield for the sake of the prospects of a devaluation of the dollar, for it seems highly probable that if ever such a devaluation should be decided upon it would be part of a co-ordinated all-round devaluation to be arranged under the auspices of the International Monetary Fund. Should that be the case, their own relatively soft currencies would be devalued simultaneously with the dollar and probably to at least the same extent. In the unlikely event of an independent devaluation of the dollar, all softer currencies, including those of the borrowing countries, would be certain to follow its example immediately, so that borrowers would not stand to gain by the dollar devaluation.

Euro-dollar rates and other Euro-currency deposit rates affect interest rates on bonds in two senses. They influence the cost of temporary financing of the transactions by issuing houses and underwriters who may employ borrowed Euro-dollars or other Euro-currencies for that purpose. We saw above that if the cost of short-term facilities is high it tends to discourage the issuing houses and underwriters from engaging in such transactions unless the terms of the loan and of the underwriting commission are such as to compensate them for the additional cost, and to enable them to unload their shares without risk of loss or delay.

The other way in which Euro-dollar rates are liable to affect bond interest rates arises from the lengthening tendency of the maturities of Euro-dollar deposits. At the time of writing it is possible to borrow Euro-dollars almost as a matter of routine up to three years, and negotiated transactions are known to have been arranged even up to five years. Conceivably some investors compare the yields of dollar bonds with those of long-term Euro-dollar deposits. Their decision whether to change into or out of bonds must depend on the differentials. As already pointed out, this need not necessarily mean that a bond issue with an average maturity of fifteen years must offer much higher yields than a five-year deposit. If holders of Euro-dollar deposits take the view that interest rates are likely to decline, so that they might not be able to renew their deposits on such favourable terms, they might be willing to accept even a lower yield than the one earned on Euro-currency deposits, since it is assured for a longer period. Moreover, they may

67

feel safe in investing in long-term bonds on the assumption that, should they require their money before the bonds mature they could always realise their investment at a profit, because of the rise in bond prices that would result from lower interest rates.

The views taken by investors on prospects of long-term Interest rates, and of the market in fixed interest bearing securities in general, are an important influence which affects equally the attractions of European dollar bonds and of foreign dollar bonds quoted in Wall Street. But any change in the level and trend of foreign bond prices in the United States might in given circumstances affect the European bonds independently of the general view taken of prospects of interest rates, because, as we saw above, these bonds compete, at any rate, to a limited extent, with European dollar bonds.

Part of the demand for European dollar bonds is by residents in countries with exchange controls who succeeded in circumventing those controls. To a by no means negligible extent, therefore, the prices of the bonds and their yields are liable to be influenced by changes and prospects of changes in exchange regulations, and even more by changes in the actual or anticipated effectiveness of their application.

As far as the United Kingdom is concerned an additional factor is the level of the premium on investment dollars. At the time of writing that premium practically rules out any demand for the bonds by U.K. residents, unless they have foreign securities which they wish to replace by such bonds, or possess investment dollars derived from the realisation of such securities. The premium on investment dollars would have to decline very considerably before its fluctuations became a factor affecting the terms of the new issues of European dollar bonds in existing circumstances. With the premium above 8 per cent at the time of writing, this contingency may appear very remote. But it is well to remember that a few years earlier the premium was quite negligible, and that the corresponding premium is quite negligible now in other financial centres, so that the possibility of its decline to a sufficiently low level to make its use for purchases of European dollar bonds a practical possibility cannot be ruled out.

The extent of competition between rival issuing houses in various financial centres is liable to affect bonds to some degree. We have already recalled above that during the 'twenties Central European and other borrowers were able to obtain unduly favourable terms because of the cut-throat competition between American and other issuing houses. At the time of writing there is very little indication of a return to those conditions, but there is enough competition to preclude the possibility of forcing unduly severe terms on eager borrowers.

Finally, the degree of attraction of alternative facilities for covering the requirements of potential borrowers is also liable to affect the terms of foreign dollar bond issues. A reason why the virtual closing down of the New York market for such issues in July 1963 did not lead to a sharper rise in interest rates on European dollar bond issues was the willingness of American banks to tide over many foreign borrowers by granting them credits for unusually long periods. The lengthening of maturities of Euro-dollar deposits also provided an alternative.

The existence of international long-term interest rates is significant from several points of view.

(1) They are apt to react on Euro-dollar rates.

(2) They are apt to react on exchange rates.

(3) They are apt to react on domestic short-term and long-term interest rates in the countries concerned.

These effects may be distinct from, and in addition to, the various direct effects of European dollar loan issues, produced through the resulting operations in foreign exchanges and Euro-currencies. We shall see below, for instance, that in addition to affecting Euro-dollar rates through borrowing of Euro-dollar deposits for the temporary financing of the transactions, or through causing the owners of such deposits to use them for acquiring dollar bonds, such transactions on a large scale are also apt to affect them through the comparison of the yields on such bonds with interest rates on long-term Euro-dollar deposits.

CHAPTER 8

IMPACT ON EURO-DOLLARS

THERE is a degree of similarity in some respects between European dollar bonds and Euro-dollars. Like Euro-dollars, these bonds constitute claims in U.S. dollars, which are actually payable in ordinary U.S. dollars in the United States, even if during the interval between borrowing and repayment the dollars involved may change hands any number of times between non-resident holders outside the United States. They represent dollar loans lent largely, though not exclusively, by non-resident holders of dollars. Their markets are mostly in Europe. Their special European character may be terminated if they are sold to an American resident, just as the European character of a Euro-dollar deposit may be terminated if it is used for payments to residents in the United States, or if its owner ceases to re-deposit it outside the United States.

There are, however, some important differences, apart altogether from the obvious one between long-term bonds and short- or medium-term deposits. When Euro-dollar deposits change hands their nominal amount is unchanged and it is only the deposit rates that are subject to the operation of the market mechanism. On the other hand, interest rates of European dollar bonds remain unchanged, but the prices at which they change hands is subject to market influences. While in the case of Euro-dollars the ultimate debtor is invariably one of the American banks with which the dollars are held on deposit, in the case of European dollar bonds the ultimate debtor is a non-resident, even if payment is to be made by the debtor in U.S. dollars, payable in the United States. Possibly payment may be made in another currency if the investor has an option to demand interest and principal in another currency.

There may of course be a substantial difference between the security of the two claims. Euro-dollar deposits are, in spite of their name, short- or medium-term credits and they are entirely unsecured. European dollar bonds, on the other hand, may or may not be secured by specific guarantees, or they may represent a definite charge on tangible assets or specific revenues. In each case there is only a single debtor whose insolvency would affect the investor, while Euro-dollar deposits may have gone through the hands of a succession of borrowers, and default by any one of them is liable to produce chain-reactions that might result in the non-payment of the debt, if a solvent debtor should be prevented by exchange restriction from securing the dollars to replace the amount he failed to receive from his defaulting debtor.

The impact of European dollar bond issues on Euro-dollar rates depends partly on the extent to which the transactions are financed by means of borrowed Euro-dollars or by means of investing Euro-dollars for that purpose by their owners, and partly on the extent to which this form of borrowing takes the place of borrowing Euro-dollar deposits. Euro-dollar rates are also liable to be influenced by the issue terms of, and subsequent yield on, European dollar bonds. Finally, they are liable to be affected indirectly by the effects of such bonds — both through the impact of their issue and through their interest rate — on the dollar rate and on local interest rates.

European dollar bonds are financed by investors to some extent with the aid of long-term Euro-dollar deposits borrowed for that purpose and renewed again and again. In Britain the authorities encourage such use of Euro-dollars by granting licences for borrowing them for periods up to twelve months for financing the acquisition of approved dollar investments. Even so, such transactions must surely be exceptional. The purpose for which borrowed Euro-dollars are used on a large scale is for the temporary financing of the transaction by issuing houses and underwriters, pending the definite placing of the bonds with investors. Euro-dollars, or for that matter any other Euro-currencies, are eminently suitable for that purpose, since issuing houses and banks of high standing that participate in under-writing can very easily borrow large amounts at a very short notice at rates that often compare favourably with the cost of alternative forms of borrowing. Such institutions may save interest by borrowing very short-term Euro-dollars and repeatedly renewing the deposits if by their maturity the bonds have not been disposed of.

European dollar bond issues are usually accompanied by a demand for Euro-dollars for such temporary financing and, perhaps to some extent, for permanent financing by investors. This temporary demand, if on a sufficiently large scale, is liable to affect Euro-dollar rates. The repayment of such credits after the bonds have been placed with investors reverses this effect. If, however, a series of bond issue transactions follow each other in close succession the effect of the repayment is offset by that of new temporary borrowing.

The institutional change of the development of the market in European dollar bonds has resulted in a once-for-all increase in the demand for Euro-dollar credits, in that a certain amount of Euro-dollars are used more or less all the time for such temporary financing even if they are repaid and re-borrowed over and over again. Any increase in the volume of European dollar bond issues, or in the delays of placing the newly issued bonds with investors, tends to cause an increase in the Euro-dollar requirements for that purpose and tends to raise Euro-dollar rates. Any decline in the volume of bond issues or a shortening of delays for unloading the bonds tends to cause a decline in the requirements of Euro-dollars for that purpose and a decline in Euro-dollar rates.

Euro-dollars are not borrowed systematically on a large scale for the purpose of a permanent financing of European dollar bonds. At the time of writing the interest differential between three years Euro-dollar deposits and even relatively short-term ten to fifteen year dollar bonds is too narrow to make it worth while for investors to finance permanently holdings of such bonds by such means. He would expose himself to the risk of having to renew the Euro-dollars at a much higher rate. Unless he holds very strong views about the likelihood of a decline in Euro-dollar rates he is not likely to take such a risk. The lower Euro-dollar rates are the higher is the risk that renewal might have to be affected at much less favourable rates.

Moreover, there is also a remote risk that, over a period of years, something might develop that would interfere with the functioning of the Euro-dollar market — such as the adoption of new exchange restrictions — so that renewal of deposits could no longer be effected as a matter of routine. Such a change might force holders to resort to some costlier method of financing or to sell their investment — possibly at an inopportune moment.

It is of course conceivable that a decline in Euro-dollar rates, or a rise in interest rates on European dollar bonds, or a combination of both, might widen the differential to a level at which it would appear worth while to take the risk attached to financing the bonds with the aid of borrowed Euro-dollars. It is also conceivable that investors might come to anticipate widely a decline in Euro-dollar rates so that they might think it worth their while to be content for a while with a narrow profit margin.

Interest rates on new dollar bond issues are liable to affect Euro-dollar rates by influencing borrowers' decisions whether or not to resort to bond issues in preference to covering their requirements with the aid of Euro-dollar credits. It also influences investors' decision whether to tie down their capital in long-term dollar bonds or hold Euro-dollar deposits on the assumption that Euro-dollar rates are more likely to rise than to decline.

While borrowers' decisions, once made, cannot be changed until they want to raise additional funds or re-finance maturing debts, investors are in a position to reach new decisions at any time. Should they decide that the differential between Euro-dollar rates and yields on existing dollar bonds make it worth their while to replace their Euro-dollar deposits by such bonds the resulting operations tend to lower yields on bonds and to raise Euro-dollar rates. Conversely, should they take the opposite view, the resulting operations tend to raise yields on bonds and to lower Euro-dollar rates.

The following is a summary of the ways in which issue of European dollar bonds tend to cause a rise in Euro-dollar rates:

(1) The transactions may involve additional temporary

financing with the aid of borrowed Euro-dollars whenever there is an excess of new temporary requirements
for that purpose over repayments of deposits previously
borrowed for that purpose.

(2) Wide differentials make it appear immediately profitable
to risk permanent financing of European dollar bond
holdings with the aid of borrowed Euro-dollar deposits
to be renewed on maturity.

(3) Narrow differentials caused by high Euro-dollar rates
may make it appear profitable in the long run to risk
permanent financing of European dollar bond holdings
with borrowed Euro-dollars on the assumption that
Euro-dollar rates are likely to fall.

(4) An appreciation of forward dollars resulting from the
beneficial effect of European dollar bond issues on the
dollar reduces the cost of borrowing Euro-dollar deposits
and stimulates, therefore, the demand for them. To put
it in a different way, a reduction in the cost of covering
the exchange risk on borrowed Euro-dollars enables
borrowers to pay higher interest rates.

The ways in which European dollar bond operations tend to
cause a decline in European dollar rates may be summarised as
follows:

(1) Borrowed Euro-dollar deposits may be repaid out of the
proceeds of European dollar bond issues.

(2) Borrowing by means of such bond issues may be resorted
to in preference to borrowing Euro-dollars.

(3) If the diversion of foreign long-term borrowing from
New York causes New York interest rates to decline, to
some extent Euro-dollar rates tend to move in sympathy.

(4) A decline in the yield on European dollar bonds tends to
cause a decline in Euro-dollar rates also by discouraging
the borrowing of Euro-dollars for the purpose of financing the issue or holding of such bonds.

It is impossible to assess even approximately the relative
extent to which the two sets of conflicting influences are liable
to affect Euro-dollar rates on balance. All we can do is to
indicate their effects in either direction and hope that later, in

possession of more experience in the working of the system, it might become possible to arrive at more definite and more helpful conclusions. As a tentative conclusion I am inclined to believe that, on balance, the European dollar bond issues, in so far as they are additional to the amount that would be issued in New York in the absence of facilities in Europe, and in so far as they constitute an alternative to borrowing of Euro-dollars tends to cause a fall in Euro-dollar rates, unless such issues are financed with the aid of Euro-dollars on a very large scale.

To what extent is the effect on Euro-dollar rates, whatever it may be, due to the choice of the dollar as the currency in which the bonds are issued? Does it modify the influence of the device on Euro-dollar rates if the European foreign bond issues do not assume the form of dollar bonds?

In so far as the effect is due to the use of the new facilities as alternatives to short- and medium-term investment in Euro-dollar deposits, possibly there would be less inducement for making the change if the bonds were in terms of some other monetary unit. Their yield is not so easily comparable with that of Euro-dollar deposits. Those wishing to remain in dollars would not be interested. Most of those inclined to switch into some other currencies would probably be influenced by considerations other than yield. If the foreign bonds issued in Europe are issued in a currency that is widely expected to be revalued — such as the D. mark at the time of writing — many investors might be inclined to accept even a lower yield than the interest on Euro-dollar deposits for the sake of the prospects of a capital profit on revaluation. The same is true, of course, in respect of bonds convertible into equities which are acquired for their prospects of capital appreciation. Safeguards against devaluation provided by the formula of the composite unit of account, and the renunciation of revaluation profit that its adoption implies, introduces yet another set of considerations influencing investors' decisions when comparing the yield of European bonds with that of Euro-dollar deposits.

The extent to which Euro-dollars are used for the temporary financing of bond issues is liable to be affected by the cost of forward covering if the bonds are in a different currency. On the other hand, the use of borrowed Euro-dollars for a permanent financing of investments in European bonds would not be affected, because investors would not be likely to cover the forward exchange.

The choice of a non-dollar currency for the denomination of the bonds reduces the extent to which the proceeds are used for repayment of Euro-dollar deposits, if the borrower envisages a devaluation of the dollar. Likewise a diversion of borrowing from the Euro-dollar market to the bond issue market would be affected by the choice of European bonds of a different denomination owing to the possibility of a revaluation or a devaluation of the currency concerned.

The effect of a diversion of foreign borrowing from the United States on the American balance of payments and, through that effect, on Euro-dollar rates, is the same whether or not the European issues are in dollars or in other currencies. The same is true about the effect of European bond issues on foreign demand for American credit facilities.

To the extent to which the effect of European dollar bond issues is favourable to the American balance of payments and, through it, to the dollar, it tends to reduce Euro-dollar rates in the following ways:

(1) By inspiring confidence in the dollar, thereby reducing demand for Euro-dollars by speculators for the purpose of selling the proceeds in order to create a short position.

(2) By strengthening the spot dollar, thereby obviating the necessity for dear money measures in its defence. Since the Euro-dollar market always tries to keep its rates below deposit rates paid in New York, this tends to cause a decline in Euro-dollar deposit rates, or at any rate it prevents an increase in Euro-dollar rates that would occur otherwise.

On the other hand, in so far as the strengthening of confidence in the dollar through the effects of European dollar bond issues tends to cause an appreciation of forward dollars it tends to increase demand for Euro-dollar credits, because of the reduction in the cost of covering the exchange risk. Since borrowers have to give away less in the form of forward dollar premium, they can afford to pay higher Euro-dollar rates.

Moreover, to the extent to which the new practice results in a reduction in the volume of Euro-dollar deposits through their consolidation into long-term indebtedness, it causes a rise in Euro-dollar rates in face of persistent unchanged demand.

Owing to the importance of this aspect of new problems, it is necessary to examine with great care the impact of dollar bond issues on the volume of Euro-dollar deposits. On the face of it, the issue of European dollar bonds must tend to reduce the turnover in the Euro-dollar market, because some deposits are immobilised through their use for financing bond holdings, and many of them are repaid out of the proceeds of the loans. On that ground it would appear that the result of the dollar bond issues is a consolidation of some of the floating funds represented by Euro-dollar deposits. After all, individual holders of such deposits do consolidate their short-term investments into long-term investments, and individual debtors owing Euro-dollars do consolidate their short-term debts into long-term debts. Obvious as these conclusions may seem at first sight, for that very reason they call for closer examination.

A reduction in the volume of Euro-dollars, whether through consolidation of investment or repayment of debts, need not be more than purely temporary, provided that there is no reduction in the overall demand for Euro-dollars. For in the Euro-dollar market, as indeed in all good markets, a two-way 'Say's Law' is in operation — supply creates its demand, but likewise demand creates its supply. If short-term investments and floating debts are consolidated to the same extent the turnover would decline. But if a consolidation of short-term investments, unaccompanied by a corresponding consolidation of short-term debts, reduces the supply of Euro-dollars available and the reduced supply meets an unchanged demand, Euro-dollar rates tend to rise. This again tends to attract additional dollars into the Euro-dollar market. Conversely, if the use of the proceeds of dollar bond issues for repayment of floating dollar debt is in excess of the amount of Euro-dollar deposits converted into long-term investment, the resulting decline in Euro-dollar rates tends to attract additional demand which again would create its supply.

Practical experience gained in a different sphere confirms the theory that demand for Euro-dollars tends to cause a replenishment of its depleted supply.   During 1963 there was a sharp reduction in the amount of dollars Central Banks had lent directly or indirectly to the Euro-dollar market.   In spite of that there was no perceptible decline in the turnover, because the effect of these withdrawals on Euro-dollar rates induced other holders of dollars, both American and non-American, to transfer funds to the Euro-dollar market.   It seems that, given the pressure of demand for Euro-dollar deposits, rates tend to become adapted to a level at which sufficient additional supply is secured to replace the supply withdrawn and meet the demand.   If certain holders or classes of holders such as Central Banks or, in the case with which we are here concerned, investors in European dollar bonds, reduce their holdings of Euro-dollar deposits other owners of dollars take their place as a result of a rise in Euro-dollar rates.

In any case, we saw above that temporary financing of bond issues tends in given circumstances to raise Euro-dollar rates. To the extent to which this occurs additional supplies may be attracted to the market, so that in spite of the consolidation of some deposits the net result of the operation is an actual increase in the total volume of Euro-dollar deposits.

The basic fact of the situation is that, owing to the low level of Euro-dollar rates compared with lending rates in most borrowing countries, potential demand for Euro-dollar credits is virtually unlimited.   Any fall in the rate would cause an increase in demand by creditworthy borrowers, which again would tend to restore rates to their original level.

European dollar bond issues may be financed not only with the aid of Euro-dollar deposits but also with the aid of any other Euro-currency deposits.   Although it is simpler for the subscriber to use Euro-dollars he already possesses in payment for the bonds and for banks to use borrowed Euro-dollars for that purpose, they might find it convenient to use Euro-sterling or other Euro-currencies. Borrowers of such currencies might sell them outright, or they might want to cover the exchange risk by swapping into dollars. Likewise, holders of Euro-currency deposits either sell their currencies against dollars or cover the exchange risk at the same time. Since forward rates tend to adjust themselves to interest parities between Euro-currencies there is usually very little advantage or disadvantage in choosing one Euro-currency in preference to another, though occasionally discrepancies which would influence their choice might arise. Or subscribers may hold deposits in one of the Euro-currencies other than Euro-dollar. Advantages from using other Euro-currencies are more pronounced when, owing to the prevailing level or prospects of the spot rates, it is not deemed necessary to cover the exchange risk when borrowing such Euro-currencies. To the extent to which Euro-currencies other than Euro-dollars are used it is of course their rates that tends to be affected by the transactions.

Conversely, Euro-dollar rates and the turnover in Euro-dollars are liable to be affected by the issue of bonds other than European dollar bonds, in so far as the transactions are financed with the aid of Euro-dollars. There is indeed no reason why issuing houses should not use Euro-dollars for financing bonds issued in terms of composite units of account or in terms of any hard currency or in terms of their local currency. Nor, for that matter, is there any particular reason why such temporary financing should not be effected in cases of domestic capital transactions of every kind. The Euro-dollar market provides very convenient facilities for such temporary financing, and Euro-dollar rates are liable to be influenced by them, regardless of whether the capital issues consist of domestic or foreign bonds or equities. This has to be borne in mind in order to avoid a misconception that the influence of foreign dollar bond issues on Euro-dollars is necessarily a special case, even though it has some special aspects.

The main difference between the impact of dollar bond issues and that of capital issues in general on Euro-dollars lies in the fact that in the case of the former there is some possibility of time arbitrage, in spite of the fact that, apart altogether from differences in the length of maturity, the two investments are far from being absolutely interchangeable.

If and when an active market should develop in European dollar bonds, speculative transactions in such bonds are liable to be financed with the aid of Euro-dollars on an extensive scale. Should such operations assume considerable dimensions the fluctuations in their volume might well affect Euro-dollar rates in the same way as spells of speculative activity in gold affected them from time to time.

CHAPTER 9

IMPACT ON THE DOLLAR EXCHANGE

THE main object of the Interest Equalisation Tax, to relieve the American balance of payments of pressure due to the excessive foreign long-term borrowing in New York, is served by the new tax partly through discouraging U.S. residents from subscribing to such loans and partly through giving European financial centres a chance to develop their capital markets for absorbing domestic and foreign capital issues which would otherwise be floated in New York. The latter object was also intended to be served by the issue of the excellent report published by the United States Treasury early in 1964, referred to in Chapter 1, providing a wealth of valuable information about the facilities, practices and comparative advantages and defects of Western European capital markets.

In taking these steps to develop capital issuing activities in Europe the U.S. authorities were doubtless aware that the resulting additional activities would assume mainly the form of foreign dollar bond issues. No doubt they had hoped that facilities would also develop for purely domestic issues in domestic currencies to cover domestic requirements, especially by France and other countries where industries and others in need of capital found it easier and cheaper to borrow in New York than in their own inadequately developed domestic capital markets.

The figures relating to foreign issues in New York prior to the change of policy give an exaggerated idea of the actual burden of long-term lending abroad on the American balance of payments. Already before the war, and again since the war, a substantial proportion of European dollar loans issued in New York was actually placed in Europe either immediately at the time of their issue or through subsequent placings and purchases. Estimates of that proportion for recent years vary between one-quarter and three-quarters of the total. Even so, the burden

81

represented by the net amount of foreign loans absorbed by the United States must have been substantial, additional as it was to a perennial adverse balance on current account.

The extent to which an expansion of European capital markets relieves pressure on the dollar depends also on the extent to which borrowers use American long-term bank credits as an alternative to making public issues in New York. This is known to have been done since the announcement of the Interest Equalisation Tax to a by no means negligible extent. To meet requirements of foreign borrowers prevented by the anticipation of that tax from issuing loans in the United States, American banks were prepared to grant credits for much longer periods than had hitherto been customary in New York.

The Euro-dollar market, too, has provided foreign long-term borrowers with facilities which are to some extent an alternative to those provided by the New York capital market. Maximum maturities of Euro-dollar deposits have become much larger since the announcement of the Interest Equalisation Tax, and the market can now provide limited facilities which, to some extent, serve as a substitute for public issues in New York. In so far as such funds had already been lent outside the United States their re-lending for longer periods does not impose any additional direct burden on the American balance of payments. In so far as such lendings replace the issues of bonds that would have been made in New York, and to the extent to which such bonds would have been actually retained in the United States, it appears on the face of it that the diversion of foreign capital issues from New York to the Euro-dollar market tends to bring relief to the dollar, at any rate in a negative sense.

The next question is in what sense and to what extent the choice of the dollar as the currency of the foreign bond issue stands to affect the dollar. The answer depends on how the dollars are raised by the lender and for what purpose they are used by the borrower. The dollars provided by issuing houses, underwriters and investors may originate in the following ways:

(1) U.S. non-residents buy dollars.
(2) U.S. non-residents employ their own Euro-dollar deposits or borrowed Euro-dollar deposits.

(3) U.S. non-residents employ their own dollar deposits or the proceeds of other realised dollar assets.

(4) U.S. residents invest funds legitimately held abroad.

(5) U.S. residents invest their existing 'refugee' funds.

(6) U.S. residents employ funds specially transferred abroad for that purpose.

Demand for dollars in the foreign exchange market by subscribers, or by issuing houses and underwriters who have to provide the amount not covered by subscribers, obviously supports the dollar exchange. If, however, subscribers are British residents and the demand is for investment dollars it does not affect the dollar exchange, except perhaps indirectly, through the psychological effect of a widening of the premium on investment dollars. If the demand is for the Dutch or Belgian equivalents of investment dollars and the Dutch or Belgian authorities support the rate, the reduction of their dollar reserves tends to strengthen the dollar potentially, without affecting its exchange rate. But if the transaction entails a transfer of foreign holdings of dollars from official reserves into private hands it may constitute a potential threat to the dollar.

The effect on the dollar exchange of the use of Euro-dollars for the purpose of subscribing to European dollar bonds is a most difficult question to answer. It is indeed hard to resist the temptation to call it 'the 64 Euro-dollar question'. We saw in the last chapter that both the temporary financing of the transaction by issuing houses and underwriters with the aid of borrowed Euro-dollars and the permanent financing of such bond holdings by investors with the aid of their Euro-dollar deposits tend to cause a rise in Euro-dollar rates. On the other hand, borrowing by issuing European dollar bonds instead of borrowing Euro-dollars, or the consolidation of Euro-dollar debts out of the proceeds of the dollar bond issues, tends to cause Euro-dollar rates to decline.

The effect of such movements of Euro-dollar rates on the dollar exchange rate is analysed in detail in my recent book, *The Euro-Dollar System*. The following are the points relevant to our present subject:

(1) An increase of Euro-dollar rates tends to attract additional funds to the Euro-dollar market. This in itself does not necessarily involve foreign exchange transactions, but if it does involve acquisition of dollars through the purchases in the foreign exchange market it affects the dollar favourably.

(2) If additional Euro-dollars are acquired temporarily by means of swap transactions the favourable effect on spot dollars is somewhat mitigated by the unfavourable effect on forward dollars. For a detailed consideration of the effects of swap transactions on forward rates and of spot rates I must refer the reader to my book *A Dynamic Theory of Forward Exchange.*

(3) An increase of Euro-dollar rates tends to affect the forward dollar unfavourably also by changing its interest parities. Forward dollars tend to adjust themselves to their interest parities between Euro-dollar and other Euro-currencies, though in actual practice it is usually the other Euro-currency rates that adjust themselves to forward dollar rates and Euro-dollar rates.

(4) Since a rise in Euro-dollar rates leaves the other interest parities of the forward dollar substantially unaffected it tends to cause an undervaluation of the forward dollar in relation to those other parities. This may give rise to outward arbitrage from New York, tending to affect the spot dollar unfavourably.

If the net effect of the European dollar bond issues on Euro-dollar rates is a decline it tends to affect the dollar in the following ways:

(1) It tends to divert dollars from the Euro-dollar market. If this assumes the form of selling dollars by owners of Euro-dollar deposits it causes a depreciation.

(2) If the dollars diverted from the Euro-dollar market are disposed of temporarily by means of swap transactions its unfavourable effect on spot dollars is somewhat mitigated by its favourable effect on forward dollars.

(3) A decline of Euro-dollar rates tends to affect the forward

dollar favourably also by changing the interest parities
between Euro-currency rates.

(4) Since a decline in Euro-dollar rates leaves the other
interest parities of the forward dollar substantially
unaffected it tends to cause an overvaluation of the
forward dollar in relation to those other parities. This
may give rise to inward arbitrage to New York, tending
to affect the spot dollar favourably.

In addition to these direct effects a rise or a decline in
Euro-dollar rates caused by European dollar bond issues are
liable to affect the dollar also indirectly. We saw in the last
chapter that the supply of Euro-dollars depleted through their
consolidation into long-term investments tends to become
replenished if the transactions cause an increase in Euro-dollar
rate. If the dollars transferred to the Euro-dollar market in
such circumstances are foreign-owned, the net result is an
unchanged external floating indebtedness of the United States
and an unchanged consolidated external indebtedness. If, on
the other hand, the additional dollars attracted to the Euro-
dollar market are American-owned it increases the gross external
floating debt position, while leaving the external consolidated
debt unchanged. The result is a weakening of the defences of
the dollar.

Another way in which a rise in Euro-dollar rates caused by
European dollar bond issues is liable to affect the dollar is by
inducing foreign holders to retain their dollars for the sake of the
higher yield. There may be many borderline cases in which
such a rise could influence decisions whether to retain dollars
or switch into other currencies. To the extent to which such an
effect is produced the operations tend to support the dollar, at
any rate in a negative sense.

If the net effect of the transaction in European dollar bonds
is a decline in Euro-dollar rates and it diverts dollars from the
Euro-dollar market, in so far as the Euro-dollars are foreign-
owned the net result is an unchanged external floating debt of
the United States and an unchanged consolidated debt. If, on
the other hand, withdrawals from the Euro-dollar market are on
American account, it reduces the gross external floating debt while

leaving the amount of external consolidated debt unchanged.

If a decline in Euro-dollar rates induces foreign holders to sell their dollars because of the inadequacy of their yield, the effect is detrimental to the dollar. In a negative sense, non-residents may decide against switching into dollars owing to the reduced yield of Euro-dollar deposits.

The investment in European dollar bonds of American funds which are already abroad — such as reserves of American subsidiaries — does not in itself affect the dollar, except possibly in a negative sense to the extent to which such bonds are acquired in preference to acquiring foreign dollar bonds issued in New York and held by residents in the United States. Such transactions would involve the purchase of dollars which does not occur if European dollar bonds are bought instead.

There is no likelihood of any new outflow of American capital for the sake of investment in foreign dollar bonds. American residents who are tempted to transfer abroad their capital in a way as to be untraceable by the fiscal authorities may or may not yield to that temptation but are guided in their decision by considerations other than any special attractions of European dollar bonds as investments.

All the effects produced on the dollar through the financing of European dollar bond issues with the aid of Euro-dollar deposits are produced also if Euro-dollar deposits are used for financing composite unit of account issues or other foreign bond issues in Europe, or indeed any domestic issues in Europe. In so far as these issues are not payable in dollars they would of course not result in any demand for dollars in the foreign exchange market that might be caused by the issue of bonds in dollar denominations. But in so far as in the absence of issuing facilities in the European capital markets such issues would have been floated in New York, their diversion to Europe relieves pressure on the dollar.

Hitherto we have been dealing with the effect of the financing of European dollar bond issues. Our next step is to examine the effect of the use made by the borrowers of the dollar proceeds. Borrowers may use their dollars for the following purposes:

(1) Repayment of outstanding dollar liabilities.
(2) Alternative financing to borrowing dollars in the United States.
(3) Alternatively financing to borrowing Euro-dollars.
(4) Payment for imports from the United States.
(5) Payment for imports from other countries.
(6) Conversion into the borrowers' local currency through the sale of the dollars in the foreign exchange market.
(7) Surrender of the dollars to the borrowers' monetary authorities.

If the proceeds are used for repayment of dollar liabilities it leaves the dollar exchange unaffected, except in a negative sense to the extent to which, in the absence of the dollar bond issues, the debtors would have had to buy dollars in the market in order to meet their liabilities. But foreign debt repayment, whether through purchases of dollars in the market or through borrowing dollars for long term from holders who are not resident in the United States, tends to strengthen the technical position of the dollar, if it reduces the American external floating debt.

We already saw above that the use of European dollar loans as an alternative to borrowing dollars in the United States tends in a negative sense, to relieve the dollar of the pressure that would be caused by such borrowing.

If borrowers cover their requirements by means of dollar bond issues instead of by means of borrowing Euro-dollar deposits, in a negative sense it tends to keep down Euro-dollar rates which would have been caused to rise as a result of such borrowing. If Euro-dollar deposits are repaid out of the proceeds of the loans the resulting decline in Euro-dollar rates would affect the dollar in a sense described above when dealing with the effects of the financing of European dollar bonds with the aid of Euro-dollars. The question is whether the sum total of the additional demand for Euro-dollars by issuing houses and underwriters and the reduction of the supply of Euro-dollars through their use by investors for subscribing to the bonds is larger or smaller than the total of repayments of Euro-dollar deposits out of the proceeds of the loan and that of the covering of requirements with the aid of dollar bond issues instead of borrowing Euro-dollars. It is the net balance that determines the effect of bond issues on Euro-dollar rates and, through them, on dollar rates.

The use of the proceeds of the dollar bond issues for payments for American exports which in the absence of such issues would have been paid through dollar purchases tends to affect the dollar unfavourably in a negative sense. But if the operation's earlier phases support the dollar in the ways described above, to that extent the negative adverse effect is cancelled out. If the U.S. exports paid for out of the proceeds of the bond issues are additional to those which would have taken place in the absence of the transactions then the favourable effects of the earlier phases of the operations will not be offset. What matters is to avoid reaching the false conclusion that the favourable effects can duplicate themselves — that the loan transactions affect the dollar favourably first through the acquisition of the dollars by the lenders and then, in addition, through their use in payment to the United States by the borrowers.

The use of the proceeds in payment for exports by other countries does not affect the dollar, unless the purchase of non-American goods is made as an alternative to purchases of American goods which would have taken place in the absence of the transaction. In that case the effect is, of course, unfavourable.

If the conversion of the proceeds of dollar bonds into local currency takes place in the open market the effect on the dollar is unfavourable. There is no such direct effect if the borrowers surrender the proceeds to their Central Banks. In that case the defences of the dollar might be affected favourably as a result of the transfer of foreign-owned dollars from private ownership to ownership by the monetary authorities, always provided that the latter are prepared to accumulate their external reserve in the form of dollars instead of availing themselves of their right to withdraw gold. On that assumption the transfer of dollars into official ownership reduces potential pressure that would arise through subsequent selling of dollars by private holders.

The dollar is affected favourably by the debtors' subsequent purchases of dollars connected with payments of interest and repayments of capital. Secondary effects of the purchases depend, however, on the ways in which interest and principal are spent by their recipients. If the receipt of the dollars obviates the necessity for them to buy dollars which they would have had to buy otherwise, the dollar rate would remain unaffected on balance.

The existence of large holdings of marketable dollar bonds held outside the United States carries the possibility of an aggravation of pressure on the dollar during periods of devaluation scares. Holders of such bonds are not quite as liable to be scared into getting out of dollars as holders of liquid dollar balances, but the difference is merely one of degree. If the buyers of the dollar bonds have to purchase the dollars, this offsets the effect of the sale of their proceeds in the foreign exchange market, but if the buyers already possess the dollars or borrow them while the sellers of the bonds sell the dollars the effect is additional selling pressure on the dollar.

Evidently the effects of European bond issues on the dollar are extremely complex and conflicting. Allowing for the negative effect produced by safeguarding the dollar against pressure due to overlending abroad, it is safe, however, to conclude that the effect is on balance distinctly favourable. The effect of the use of the dollar as the currency in which the loans are issued is also favourable, on balance, to the dollar. Apart from other considerations the fact that the new device has provided the dollar with an additional international use should work in its favour, at any rate in the absence of abnormal circumstances.

Although the effect of European issue of dollar bonds on the dollar is of outstanding importance, it is necessary to examine also their effects on other exchanges. The effects of such transactions on the exchanges of the borrowing countries are too obvious to call for detailed analysis, and so are the effects on the exchanges of the investing countries. But the effect on the exchanges of entrepôt markets deserve some attention. This subject was already touched upon in Chapter 5.

Sterling is liable to be affected by the issue of dollar bonds in London — or, for that matter, in other similarly placed centres — in the following circumstances:

(1) If non-resident sterling is converted into dollars in order to subscribe to the new issues.

(2) If non-residents realise their holdings of sterling securities and sell the proceeds against dollars on the security sterling market. Although such transactions only affect the security sterling rate, a widening of the discount on security sterling would entail the following adverse effects on sterling:

    (*a*) It would create an unfavourable psychological effect.

    (*b*) It would encourage the use of security sterling for direct investment in the United Kingdom and to that extent it would reduce demand for sterling.

    (*c*) Should the discount widen considerably it would increase the temptation for evading exchange control by non-resident holders of sterling securities.

(3) If residents subscribe with the aid of investment dollars the resulting widening of the premium on investment dollars would create an unfavourable psychological effect, and it would increase the temptation for U.K. residents to evade the exchange control.

(4) If non-residents subscribe with the aid of borrowed Euro-sterling the resulting increase in Euro-sterling rates would tend to cause a depreciation of forward sterling. The extent of that effect would be, however, purely marginal because, more often than not, Euro-sterling rates adapt themselves to Euro-dollar rates and forward sterling rates rather than influence the latter.

(5) If non-residents subscribe with the aid of borrowed Euro-dollars or if they employ their own Euro-dollars for financing their holdings of dollar bonds the resulting rise in Euro-dollar rates would cause an appreciation of forward sterling, unless Euro-sterling rates adapt themselves to the changes in Euro-dollar rates.

(6) The direct and indirect effect of the dollar bond transaction on British invisible exports tends to benefit sterling to a minor degree.

(7) Any favourable effect of the transactions on the dollar is liable to be at the expense of sterling to some extent, even if the funds are provided by foreign investors out of resources other than non-resident sterling accounts or borrowed Euro-sterling.

On balance the adverse effect on sterling, if any, is likely to be moderate, and in given circumstances the effect may be favourable. If currencies other than dollars are employed the effect is marginally more likely to be favourable, or it is likely to be marginally less unfavourable.

CHAPTER 10

IMPACT ON DOMESTIC INTEREST RATES

WE saw in Chapter 6 how domestic interest rates in the United States, in the countries where European dollar bonds are issued, in countries which took up these bonds, and in borrowing countries are liable to affect the long-term international interest rates represented by the issue terms of, and subsequent yield on, European dollar bonds. The effect is, however, reciprocal. The present chapter is to examine how such international long-term interest rates are liable to affect domestic interest rates in the United States and in the other countries concerned. Up to the time of writing the volume of the foreign dollar bond issues in Europe has not been sufficiently large to produce any noticeable positive effect on domestic interest rates, except perhaps on those of borrowing countries. Since, however, it is reasonable to envisage the possibility of an expansion in the volume of such bond issues it is necessary to examine also its probable effect on domestic interest rates in other countries.

First of all, we must inquire into the ways in which issues of European dollar bonds tend to affect the domestic interest structure in the United States. The basic fact of the situation is that the American bond market is immensely wide. Because of this, in spite of any conceivable increase in the issuing activity of dollar bonds in Europe, it cannot ever be more than a small fraction of the bond issuing activity in the United States, and any conceivable turnover in such bonds cannot ever be more than an infinitesimal fraction of the turnover in the entire American bond market. The extent to which European issues could conceivably compete for the immense volume of American capital invested or is available for investment in bonds is quite negligible. For this reason it would appear that any direct influence of interest rates or yield of dollar bonds in Europe on interest rates or yields of dollar bonds in general in the United States must always be purely marginal. The tip of the tail is not likely to move the dog to any perceptible extent.

The one section of the American bond market in which there is a possibility of a noteworthy direct effect is the market for foreign dollar bonds. Although such bonds are quoted in Wall Street, their main market is over the counter. European dollar bonds compete with these bonds, at any rate to the relatively moderate extent to which residents in the United States are in a position to invest in European dollar bonds without coming under the provisions of the Interest Equalisation Tax. European dollar bonds issued before the announcement of that tax are not subject to that tax and would offer, therefore, advantages as an alternative investment for American residents should their yields decline below those of corresponding New York issues.

There are, however, indirect ways in which the actual issue of European dollar bonds, rather than their terms of issue or the subsequent yield on those issues, is liable to affect domestic interest rates in the United States.

(1) They relieve pressure on the dollar. We saw in Chapter 9 that, although the impact of European dollar bond issues on the dollar rate is highly involved and obscure, it stands to reason that on balance the diversion of foreign borrowing from New York does tend to benefit the dollar exchange. To the extent to which it does, it obviates the need for defending the dollar by means of high interest rates or other disinflationary measures leading to a rise of domestic interest rates in the United States. In this respect foreign non-dollar issues in Europe tend to produce the same effect as dollar issues. What matters is that foreign long-term borrowing is diverted from New York.

(2) To the extent to which lending abroad would result in a drain on the gold reserve and would reduce domestic liquidity the diversion of foreign capital issues from New York to other capital markets makes for more plentiful credit and capital resources within the United States — if only in a negative sense. But in view of the

immense capital resources and domestic capital requirements of the United States, the difference is not likely to be very large.

(3) They affect Euro-dollar rates. We saw in Chapter 8 how issuing of dollar bonds in Europe tends to influence Euro-dollar rates. The latter in turn exert some degree of influence on the domestic interest structure in the United States. This is a highly involved process and for details I must refer the reader to my book *The Euro-Dollar System: Practice and Theory of International Interest Rates*, Chapter 11, which shows that Euro-dollar rates affect American domestic interest rates in the following ways:

(*a*) Through competition of Euro-dollar facilities with American short-term dollar investment or borrowing facilities.

(*b*) Through providing additional and alternative facilities for speculating against the dollar.

(*c*) Through providing additional facilities for inward or outward arbitrage.

(*d*) Through influencing the relationship between various maturities within the national interest structure.

(*e*) Through influencing official monetary policies.

These effects are highly involved and obscure and to a large extent they are liable to cancel each other out. Whether the net effect of the issuing of dollar bonds in Europe is a rise or a fall in Euro-dollar rates, it tends to react on American domestic short-term interest rates. A rise in Euro-dollar rates is particularly liable to affect the American domestic interest structure if it is sufficiently pronounced to attract substantial additional American funds to the Euro-dollar market. American banks may want to outbid Euro-dollar rates — in so far as they are permitted to do so under Regulation Q — by paying higher deposit rates. It is probably in this respect that the effect of European dollar bond issues on American interest rates can be the most pronounced. But we saw in Chapter 8 that extensive use

of the proceeds of such loans for repayment of Euro-
dollar deposits or for avoiding the borrowing of such
deposits can neutralise, and more than neutralise, the
effect of using Euro-dollars for temporary or permanent
financing of the bond issues.

(4) They affect domestic interest rates abroad. We shall
try to examine below how and to what extent dollar
bond issuing activity in Europe is liable to affect
domestic interest rates in the issuing countries, the
investing countries and in the borrowing countries. In
given circumstances changes in interest rates in these
countries may react to some extent on American
domestic interest rates, especially on short-term interest
rates. The pressure exerted by the United States
Government in 1964 on European Governments to
prevent Bank rate increases in order that interest rates
in the United States could be kept down shows how
sensitive the American interest structure is to changes in
European interest rates.

The next step is to investigate the effects on domestic interest rates in countries whose banks participate in the issue of
European dollar bonds but whose residents are prevented by the
exchange control from acquiring such issues for investment,
except with the aid of investment dollar types of currencies —
the proceeds of foreign securities realised by other holders
resident in the same country. The effects on domestic interest
rates in the United Kingdom of such issues made in London are
produced in the following ways:

(1) Through sales of non-resident sterling balances against
dollars bought for subscribing to such issues. If the
resulting weakness of sterling necessitates official
intervention leading to a decline of the gold reserve, the
authorities may have to take steps to defend sterling
by means of higher interest rates. This more than
offsets the decline in interest rates resulting from a
reduction in the volume of Treasury bill issues brought
about by the realisation of gold holdings hitherto financed by the issue of Treasury bills.

(2) Through diverting non-resident sterling from loans to the London money market, to local authorities, to hire-purchase finance houses, etc., and from investment in sterling bills. If large amounts of non-resident sterling are used by subscribers to the new dollar bonds the reduction in the supply of such foreign funds available for the above purposes might affect British domestic interest rates on a broad front. The most obvious instance is the effect produced on Treasury bill rates by a decline in the amount of tenders on foreign account, that would be brought about by a diversion of foreign funds into the market of new foreign dollar bond issues.

(3) Through its effect on Euro-dollar rates. This should tend to affect forward sterling rates — though, as we saw in the last chapter, that effect is purely marginal — and through them short-term interest rates in London.

(4) Through its effect on Euro-sterling rates which would rise if much Euro-sterling is invested in dollar bonds and if the new owners of such sterling do not wish to employ their funds in the Euro-sterling market.

(5) Through its effect on inter-bank sterling rates, if the financing of the transactions involves much direct borrowing between London banks.

(6) Through its effect on domestic interest rates in the United States, in investing countries and in borrowing countries. Changes in those rates are apt to react on British domestic interest rates.

(7) Through competing with foreign sterling bonds in London. Having regard to the present extent of foreign investors' preference for dollar bonds, the differential in favour of dollar bonds is remarkably narrow. This is because of the local demand for sterling bonds by U.K. residents who are not permitted to acquire new dollar bonds except with the aid of investment dollars quoted at a high premium.

Domestic interest rates in European countries whose residents actually acquire European dollar bonds as investments, whether or not those bonds were issued in their countries, are affected in the following ways:

(1) Through competing with alternative domestic long-term investment facilities. While primarily it is the existing foreign dollar bonds already available in Europe that are affected, if the amount of the new issues is large and the local bond market is relatively narrow, long-term interest rates in general might be affected.

(2) Through the effect on short-term interest rates of demand for credit facilities for a temporary financing of dollar bond issues.

(3) Through the effect on Euro-dollar or other Euro-currency rates of borrowing Euro-currency deposits for the temporary financing of dollar bond issues, or their use for financing permanently investments in such bonds, or through replacement of Euro-dollar deposits by dollar bonds as investments by their owners.

(4) Through the effect on exchange rates. To the extent to which pressure is diverted from the dollar it is diverted to some other currency whose weakness is liable to lead to higher local interest rates if the monetary authorities concerned defend their exchange by means of higher interest rates or credit restrictions.

(5) Through repercussions of the effect on interest rates in the United States, in the issuing countries and in borrowing countries.

Finally, we must examine the effect on the domestic interest structure in the borrowing countries themselves. This effect tends to be more pronounced than those on domestic interest rates in the United States, in issuing countries or in investing countries, because the chances are that the amounts involved represent a larger percentage of the borrowing countries' total capital market resources. Their interest rates are influenced in the following ways:

(1) Through increasing the volume of capital and through competing with local lenders. In countries which are particularly short of capital the effect of borrowing abroad is apt to be particularly pronounced.

(2) Through enabling the monetary authorities to expand credit if the dollar proceeds are acquired by the Central Bank, either direct from the borrower or through purchases in the foreign exchange market to prevent the national exchange from appreciating above support point or above any level at which the authorities want to hold it in face of the buying pressure caused by the sale of the proceeds of the dollar bonds.

(3) Through the effect on domestic interest rates of an appreciation of the borrower country's spot or forward exchange resulting from the sale of the proceeds of the bond issues and from the confidence inspired by an increase of the official dollar reserve.

(4) Through the effect on Euro-dollar rates and other Euro-currencies produced by a reduction in the demand for Euro-dollar credits.

(5) Through repercussions of the effect on interest rates in the United States, in issuing countries and in investing countries.

Possibly if and when the turnover in the market for dollar bond issues should assume considerable dimensions it might affect long-term interest rates to an appreciable extent, though to an extent inferior to the effect of trends in the Euro-dollar market on short-term interest rates. While, however, the latter tends to reduce differentials between domestic short-term interest rates in various countries, European dollar bond issues may not have such clear-cut effects on the differentials between long-term interest rates in various countries. It is true, like Euro-dollars, they assist in the international redistribution of capital resources. This need not necessarily mean, however, a reduction in differentials between domestic long-term interest rates.

If the development of this market assists the United States in maintaining low domestic interest rates, then any reduction of the differentials has to take place entirely through a reduction of interest rates in other countries. In the case of Euro-dollars the reduction of differentials is the combined effect of declining local interest rates abroad and rising interest rates in the United

States. But an increase in the volume of foreign issues in London, Paris or Frankfurt would tend to raise long term interest rates in these markets, even though they are already appreciably higher than those prevailing in New York. It is only an increase in foreign issuing activity in Amsterdam and Zürich that would tend to reduce long-term interest differentials by raising the low long-term rates in those two markets.

CHAPTER 11

COMPOSITE UNIT OF ACCOUNT LOANS

ALTHOUGH this book is primarily concerned with foreign lending in the form of bonds issued in Europe in denomination of U.S. dollars, an account of the system which it tries to cover would not be complete without a brief description and analysis of the main alternative devices — the issue of foreign loans in terms of other hard currencies, multiple currency bonds, parallel issues and, above all, composite unit of account bonds. The latter in particular has attracted much interest as an imaginative experiment. The idea of some form of international currency has long tempted imaginative economists and has given rise to proposals for the creation of international currencies circulating in a great many countries or serving as international liquid reserves. The international unit of account with which we are concerned here has no such ambitious aim. Nor is it meant to become a currency in which foreign trade would be transacted but is merely an abstract unit in terms of which international loans can be issued. In one respect it is superior to the various international currency proposals — it is actually in use, while most other suggestions are never likely to achieve concrete existence.

Before dealing with this device, we must consider loans issued in terms of currencies other than the dollar. In recent years some issues were made in sterling, mostly for borrowers in the Sterling Area but also for countries of the EFTA. The total of such loans to countries outside the Sterling Area unless they serve for re-financing maturing debt or for financing British exports — is necessarily limited by the inescapable facts of the balance of payments position. Recurrent sterling scares made such bonds appear unattractive for many non-residents, unless borrowers were prepared to offer a sufficiently high yield to compensate the risk — real or imaginary — involved in holding long-term sterling. The entire burden of such capital issues would fall on the British balance of payments — unless the authorities stipulate that only non-resident sterling can be used.

A large number of loans were issued in guilders, Swiss francs and, since 1963, in D. marks. But while devaluation rumours frequently deterred many investors from taking an interest in sterling bonds, revaluation rumours that persistently recurred from time to time discouraged many borrowers from incurring long-term liabilities in terms of these currencies. The low interest rates in the Swiss and Dutch bond markets offered some inducement to would-be borrowers, but long-term rates in Germany remained uncompetitive until the exemption of foreign D. mark bonds from the Yield Tax imposed on non-resident investors made them attractive as a means for speculation on D. mark revaluation. In consequence of the resulting foreign demand it became possible to issue such bonds on acceptable terms. It is estimated that something like 70 per cent of the bonds are taken up outside Germany.

An alternative solution to the issue of bonds in a hard currency would be to revert to the formula of gold clause that was fashionable in the 'twenties. In several European countries the issue of loans with a gold clause is, however, unlawful. In any case, the experience with gold clauses in American dollar issues, which were cancelled by legislation in 1933, is still remembered and investors are not very keen on the formula. The banks engaged in the elaboration of the terms of European bond issues prefer, therefore, to avoid the insertion of any provision that would amount to a gold clause.

Ever since 1957 Continental banks have been experimenting with loans comprising some form of 'multiple currency clause' under which bondholders can claim payment of interest and principal in any one of several currencies, on the basis of fixed exchange rates, usually the exchange parities prevailing at the time of the issue. For instance, in 1957 a Belgian oil company issued in Canada, Switzerland, Belgium, Germany and Holland a twenty-year loan of $25 million containing a clause providing for payment in guilders, D. marks, Swiss francs or Belgian francs at a fixed exchange rate, at the bondholders' option. This transaction was followed by a number of others based on the same principle. But the formula was not looked upon as satisfactory by many borrowers. Those in a position to refuse to sign on the dotted line declined it because it would mean that, should any one of the currencies of the contract be revalued, all bondholders would claim payment in that currency. The debtor would suffer a loss, without a corresponding chance to gain by devaluation unless all the currencies of the contract were devalued. A devaluation of the debtors' own currency would mean a corresponding increase in the burden of his debt.

A mitigated form of currency option enables investors to choose between several currencies at the time when the loan is issued. Once he has made his choice, however, he is not in a position to alter it. This formula does not entail anything like the same risk for the borrower as the multiple currency clause. Nor does it provide anything like the same safeguard for the lender.

Dr. Hermann Abs, head of the Deutsche Bank, advocated the issue of 'parallel' loans in several national tranches each of which would be in the currency of the market in which it is issued. The interest rate on all tranches would be uniform, but the issue prices would vary according to the conditions prevailing in the various markets. Although the plan has its good points it does not seem to have been received favourably. It would not solve the problem of integrating the European capital markets, because bonds issued in terms of various European currencies would be judged by investors according to the view they take of the currencies in which they are issued, and price differentials would tend to remain.

One of the difficulties of parallel issues would be the difficulty of synchronising their issue. Owing to the discrepancies between regulations in various countries relating to new issues of foreign bonds, and also between the actual application of those regulations in practice, there may have to be time lags of a month or more between the various issues, and meanwhile interest rates are liable to change.

Having regard to the disadvantages of the various alternative schemes, it is not surprising that the formula of issuing bonds in terms of composite units of account should meet with favourable response. It was first put forward by a Belgian banker, M. F. Collin, and was first applied in actual practice in 1961. It seeks to reconcile the conflicting interests of borrowers and lenders. Loans issued in terms of composite units of account differ from multiple currency loans in that the creditor has no option to choose among the 'reference currencies' but has to be content with receiving payment in that of these currencies which has not appreciated or depreciated, or which has depreciated or appreciated to the least extent. This formula reduces to a minimum losses debtors are liable to suffer through revaluations, because the list of reference currencies contains some which are most unlikely to be revalued. It also reduces to a minimum losses lenders are liable to suffer through devaluations, because some of the reference currencies are most unlikely to be devalued. It seeks to ensure that payment of interest and repayment of capital is made in a monetary unit whose gold value corresponds as nearly as possible to that of the one in which the loan was made.

The composite unit of account is based on the system elaborated under the European Payments Union Scheme in 1950 for the purpose of clearing debit and credit items between members of the Union through the Bank for International Settlements. Details of the EPU system are highly involved and need not concern us here, especially as its use was discontinued with the termination of the EPU. M. Collin's formula took over from the EPU system the list of reference currencies which formed the basis of loan contracts. Details of the actual application of this formula vary from issue to issue, but the fundamental rule that, while the currency in which the debtor has to discharge payments is left to the choice of the creditor, the exchange rate on the basis of which payment is made in the currency chosen must be the one which is the nearest to the original exchange parities as defined in the contract, is embodied in all contracts. Creditors are not entitled to benefit by revaluations unless and until all seventeen currencies have been revalued, and even then their payment is to be made on the basis of the currency which is revalued to the smallest extent. In the absence of changes in the legal parities, or if floating exchange rates are adopted, payment is made on the basis of the currency which has appreciated to the smallest extent.

In their turn, debtors can only benefit by devaluation if all seventeen currencies are devalued or depreciated, and even then this benefit would be based on the devaluation or depreciation of the currency which was devalued or which depreciated to the smallest extent.

If only some of the reference currencies are revalued or devalued, the payment in the currency chosen by the bond-holders has to be reckoned on the basis of the exchange rate of one of the currencies which are not revalued or devalued. So long as there remains one single reference currency out of the seventeen which is not revalued or devalued, or which, in the absence of legal changes in its parity, has not depreciated or appreciated, the bondholders are safeguarded against exchange loss and are deprived of exchange profit. This formula does not provide an absolutely watertight safeguard for investors against a devaluation of the currency of the investment, but devaluation risk is greatly reduced. Indeed it could not be reduced even more without the application of some provision which would amount to a gold clause pure and simple. On the other hand, prospects of a revaluation profit are also reduced to a minimum. Non-speculative investors gladly pay that price for the safeguard against devaluation.

The formula does not of course safeguard debtors against the risk of a loss through a devaluation of their own currency, nor does it deprive debtors of profit through a revaluation of their own currency. If the debtors' own currency is one of the seventeen reference currencies the only situation in which, in case of a devaluation or revaluation of all currencies, it becomes the currency of the payments under the loan contract is if the extent of its change is smaller than that of all other reference currencies. Otherwise payments have to be made in another currency, in which case the debtor benefits by an appreciation of his currency in terms of that currency and suffers a loss through a depreciation of his own currency in terms of that currency. The rule applies in reverse to creditors and their currencies. The formula does not safeguard them from loss through a revaluation of their own currency, nor does it deprive them of profits from a devaluation of their own currency, unless their currency becomes the currency of the payments under the loan contract.

Complications arise if some of the seventeen currencies are devalued while others are revalued. Under the original formula some anamolous situations were liable to arise. If, for instance, sixteen reference currencies were devalued substantially while one was revalued slightly, payment would be made on the basis on the one revalued currency, in conformity with the provision that the payment has to be based on the value of the reference currency whose departure from the basic parities is the smallest. Conversely, if sixteen currencies were drastically revalued while the seventeenth moderately devalued, creditors would suffer a disadvantage, because payment would be made on the basis of the lower value of the one devalued currency, even if that currency were the least important among the reference currencies.

A more equitable formula has therefore been adopted, according to which the unit of account has to be changed only if all seventeen reference currencies have been either devalued or revalued, and it has to be changed in the same direction in which two-thirds of the currencies have changed, but only to the extent of the change in the currency that has changed to the least extent in that direction. This means that if at least twelve out of the seventeen currencies have been changed in the same direction while five or fewer currencies have been changed in the opposite direction, the currency whose new value must form the basis of payments is the one of the majority which has changed to the smallest extent.

This solution is far from being ideal. For one thing, it is not applied if eleven or less currencies are changed in the same direction, even though such a situation would result in the application of the self-same absurd anomalous solution that has been criticised above. The formula is also criticised for being complicated and unintelligible far beyond the understanding of the ordinary investor who, after all, has to make up his mind on its merits and demerits in order to decide whether to acquire and hold bonds based on it.   Finally, it has also been criticised on the ground that some of the seventeen reference currencies are quite unimportant and therefore at best irrelevant and at worse detrimental to the interests of creditors or debtors.   This may best be judged by glancing at the following list of them and their parities or 'basic values':

One unit of account is equal to one U.S. dollar and to

26·000 Austrian schillings
50·000 Belgian francs
6·907 Danish kroner
4·000 German D. marks
0·357 pounds sterling
30·000 Greek drachmae
43·000 Icelandic kroner
0·357 Irish pounds
625·001 Italian lire
50·000 Luxembourg francs
3·620 Netherlands guilders
7·143 Norwegian kroner
28·749 Portuguese escudos
5·173 Swedish kronor
4·373 Swiss francs
9·000 Turkish pounds

All these parities are identical with those of the U.S. dollar in relation to the seventeen currencies, so that the unit of account is equal to one dollar at its present gold weight and fineness.   A change in the gold content of the dollar would not affect the parities, for the unit of account would remain based on the quantity of gold represented by the dollar since its devaluation in 1934 — 0·88867088 grammes of fine gold.   But if, as is probable, a dollar devaluation should be followed by a series of devaluations of all reference currencies it would affect the gold value of the currency in which payment must be made, which would become adjusted to the value of the reference currency whose devaluation would be the smallest.

The prices of unit of account bonds would be affected by

trends in exchange rates if there appeared to be a possibility of changes in all parities. For instance, if a devaluation of all reference currencies were expected, the market would discount a depreciation corresponding to the anticipated extent of the devaluation of the currency which would be expected to be devalued to the smallest extent. The prices of bonds are also affected, however, by an anticipation of a possible devaluation or revaluation of at least 12 of the 17 currencies, if ever such a contingency should appear to have come within the realm of practical possibility, on the assumption that changes in the parities of the remaining currencies in either direction would lead to the adjustment of the unit of account.

Obviously the inclusion of currencies such as the Greek drachma or the Turkish pound reduces the chances of an all-round revaluation to vanishing point, so that to that extent at any rate the formula tends to safeguard the interests of the debtor. On the other hand, the inclusion of all Western European hard currencies rules out the likelihood of an all-round devaluation — except conceivably an all all-round uniform cut under the auspices of the International Monetary Fund — so that to that extent it safeguards the interests of creditors. Since, however, devaluation or revaluation of 12 out of 17 reference currencies is sufficient, provided that all remaining parities change — if, for instance, 12 softer currencies are devalued and the 5 hardest currencies are revalued — neither safeguard is absolutely watertight.

The explanation of the inclusion of soft currencies or insignificant currencies in the formula is that they had been included in the European Payments Union formula which had been accepted by all participating countries. The maintenance of that formula unchanged gives therefore the unit of account additional prestige and, as M. Collin pointed out, it greatly reduces the likelihood of legislation in any of the seventeen countries concerned against its application in loan contracts.

The objection of the Swiss authorities to the inclusion of the Swiss franc among the reference currencies was overcome as a result of an agreed compromise under which bondholders shall be entitled to be paid on the basis of the current exchange rate of the Swiss franc, but no actual payment must be made in that currency. Bondholders have to indicate their second choice of the reference currency in which the actual payment, reckoned on the basis of the current exchange rate of the Swiss franc, is to be made to them.

The attitude of the Swiss authorities is inspired by their determination to resist an extension of the use of the Swiss franc as an international currency. This attitude has obvious practical justification in so far as it aims at preventing the issue of loans abroad in terms of Swiss francs, for interest rates on such bonds necessarily compete with interest rates on similar issues in the Swiss market. As we remarked before, any conceivable total of dollar bonds issued abroad could never be more than a small fraction of the total dollar bonds issues in the United States. But in the case of Switzerland the relative proportion of Swiss franc loans issued abroad to those issued in the domestic market might well become uncomfortably high. Extensive use of the Swiss franc, even if it be through its inclusion in multiple currency clauses, or among reference currencies of unit of account issues, might conceivably influence long-term interest rates in Switzerland in a sense conflicting to official policy. Many investors might well prefer such bonds to Swiss franc bonds issued in the domestic market at lower interest rates.

Viewed from this angle, however, it seems that the Swiss authorities, in agreeing to the compromise outlined above, mistook the shadow for the substance. Investors who trust the Swiss franc implicitly might be attracted by unit of account bonds because under the new formula they are safeguarded against devaluation at least to the same extent as if they acquired Swiss franc bonds issued in Switzerland. It is true, under the terms of the compromise Swiss francs cannot be used in actual payment to bondholders. But there is nothing to prevent those receiving payments in some other currency from converting the amount received immediately into Swiss francs. They would receive the same amount of Swiss francs (less a small turn on the foreign exchange transaction) as if they had been permitted to receive actual payment in Swiss francs direct from the paying agents. In practice the paying agents may themselves carry out the conversion, in which case the actual payment would be made in Swiss francs even if no paying agents can be appointed in Switzerland.

This compromise further complicated a formula which was criticised for being over-involved even before this additional complication. Should other countries follow the Swiss example the adoption of further compromises on different terms might well reduce the system to absurdity by making it entirely unintelligible to the average investors, or even to institutional investors who are usually the principal subscribers to unit of account issues.

In any case the system has yet to face its ultimate test consisting of its interpretation by law courts. Owing to its novelty and its complicated nature, it is believed in many quarters that it is almost certain to give rise to legal actions sooner or later. In case of unforeseen contingencies legal battles would have to be fought out before Law Courts in a number of countries and new chapters would have to be added to textbooks on international law in respect of money and banking. The result of such legal battles, or the operation of the system over a prolonged period without giving rise to such lawsuits, will determine the definitive interpretation of the formula.

Subscribers to unit of account issues usually have the choice between paying in one of several currencies. This option does not extend over the full range of the seventeen reference currencies but is confined to the leading currencies.

Let us now examine the broader economic aspects of unit of account loans. In so far as they appeal to a class of borrowers, finance houses and investors who for some reason fight shy of international loans in terms of any existing currency, or in terms of the other formulas referred to above, the adoption of the new device is to be welcomed as an additional means for furthering the international redistribution of capital. So long as there are revaluation risks and devaluation risks any formula that reduces them is a welcome contribution to the solution of the problem. Time alone will show whether the contribution made by the composite unit of account formula will be able to assist to any considerable extent in the elimination of currency uncertainty as one of the main obstacles to international capital movements.

To the extent to which unit of account loans take the place of dollar loans the device tends to reduce the international use of the dollar. Until comparatively recently this might have influenced American opinion against such loans. As a result of experience during the late 'fifties and early 'sixties, it has come to be realised that the use of any one currency as an international currency has its disadvantages as well as its advantages and it would be a mistake to overrate the latter and ignore the former for misplaced considerations of prestige.

Our next task is to examine how unit of account loans affect the dollar and the other exchanges concerned. The view is widely held even in banking circles that loans issued in terms of units of account, or indeed in terms of any currency other than the dollar outside the United States, does not affect the dollar. After all, the loans are issued in the foreign market, they are not in U.S. dollar denominations, and they are lent by non-residents in the United States to non-residents in the United States. On the face of it the dollar does not come into it at all, unless American refugee funds are used by subscribers to unit of account loans and are exported for the purpose of acquiring unit of account loans. To some extent this might occur, since the unit of account formula provides a new kind of security which might possibly appeal to some American investors.

Appearances are often deceptive, however. As we pointed out already in Chapter 9, unit of account loans, as indeed loans issued in any currency other than the dollar, are liable to affect the dollar exchange. They can do so in the following ways:

(1) Holders of dollars (resident or non-resident) may sell dollars to buy the currency in which payment for the bonds have to be made.

(2) The issue or the acquisition of the bonds by investors may be financed with the aid of dollars borrowed in the United States.

(3) It may be financed with the aid of borrowed Euro-dollars.

110

(4) The proceeds may be spent on repaying debts owed in the United States.

(5) The proceeds may be spent on imports from the United States.

(6) The proceeds may be spent on non-American goods instead of importing American goods.

(7) The transaction may obviate the necessity to borrow in the United States.

From the above list it appears that dollars are by no means immune from the effect of an increase in the volume of unit of account issues. Indeed, in so far as they substitute buying of other currencies for buying of dollars by subscribers the effect may be less favourable to the dollars.

The issue of unit of account loans also affects some, but by no means all, reference currencies. There is no reason whatsoever why it should affect the less important currencies included in the list, since they are not likely ever to be chosen by the bondholders as the currency of payment. It stands to reason that lenders select the currency which they consider the best.

Let us assume for the sake of argument that the French franc is selected. In that case the franc is affected by the transaction in the following ways:

(1) There will be a demand for francs by subscribers.

(2) If the amount is not fully covered there will be a demand for francs by issuing houses and underwriters.

(3) Euro-francs may be borrowed to finance the transaction.

(4) Franc holdings may be used by investors to acquire the bonds.

(5) The franc proceeds may be sold by the borrower in order to acquire the currency they require.

(6) The francs thus sold may be acquired by the Central Bank of the borrowing country.

(7) The borrower may repay outstanding obligations in francs.

(8) The proceeds may be spent on imports from France.

(9) When interest for repayment is due francs may be acquired for that purpose.

The transaction is liable to affect also the exchanges of

countries in which unit of account loans are issued in the same way as they are affected by the issue of dollar loans. Likewise, in countries with exchange restrictions in which there is a special market for currencies that can be used for that purpose, such as the British market in investment dollars, they tend to affect the rate for such currencies in the same way as they are affected by the issue of dollar loans.

If a sufficient number of unit of account loans is issued it will create a set of international interst rates comparable to that created through the issue of European dollar loans. In theory this set of interest rates is even more international in character than the one prevailing in the market for dollar loans, which is influenced, to some extent at any rate, by interest rates prevailing in the American bond market. In practice, however, it will not be completely independent. In the course of time some sort of differential is bound to develop between the yields on unit of account bonds and those on European dollar bonds. Since the latter are in some measure influenced by domestic American interest rates the former are also liable to be affected by them indirectly.

For instance if short-term interest rates in the United States are reduced it will become more profitable for many foreign borrowers to secure credits in New York instead of issuing dollar bonds. The resulting decline in the demand for loans in the form of dollar bonds will tend to lower their interest rates and this again will tend to react on interest rates on unit of account issues. In any case, it is possible that lower short-term rates in New York might divert into that market some borrowers who would otherwise have borrowed in the form of unit of account bonds.

One of the economic advantages of dollar bonds is that in conjunction with the Euro-dollar market they establish a very useful communicating channel between long-term and short-term loans. That advantage does not exist as far as unit of account loans are concerned because there is no market in short-term unit of account credits. While it is not inconceivable that sooner or later the unit of account might be used also for short-term lending, it does not appear likely.

From the above analysis it appears that, as far as the effects of unit of account loans on exchange rates and interest rates are concerned, we are if anything even more in the realm of conjecture as in respect of the effects of European dollar loans. Should a really active market develop in unit of account loans their interest rates might well become an important factor affecting not only other international interest rates but even domestic interest rates. This is particularly true concerning interest rates in smaller countries. Hence the determination of the Swiss authorities not to allow the Swiss francs to be used among the unit of account loans.

CHAPTER 12

THE MARKET IN INVESTMENT DOLLARS

THE continued existence of the system to be described in this chapter depends on the maintenance of the exchange control measures regulating it substantially in their present form. Its operation does not affect the balance of payments. Nevertheless, it is conceivable that the British Government might adopt measures that would bring the market in investment dollars to an end. Even in that case I do not consider it a waste of time and effort to study the working of the system. It exists in substantially the same form in at least two other countries, and in Britain, too, it might conceivably be restored if and when it should be realised that its elimination served no useful purpose.

From an American point of view investment dollars differ in no way from ordinary U.S. dollars. Both are dollars deposited by residents in the United Kingdom with a bank in the United States. They are completely indistinguishable under United States law or practice. The difference arises from the British exchange control regulations under which it is only investment dollars that can be used by U.K. residents for the acquisition of dollar securities or other foreign securities. They have to be declared as such in returns submitted by dealers to the Bank of England. Their holders are entitled to sell them as ordinary dollars and for this reason investment dollars could never go to a discount. They are usually, though not necessarily, at a substantial premium, precisely because they can be used for purposes for which ordinary dollars could not be used. Investment dollars, together with security sterling, have not been affected so far by the gradual re-unification of the multiple exchange rates that developed during and after the war.

At the time of writing, British residents do not find it worth while to subscribe to European dollar bonds with the aid of investment dollars, unless they are debentures convertible into equities or unless investors want to sell some existing foreign security holdings and can thus obtain investment dollars without having to buy them. Even then they are likely to prefer to sell their investment dollars or to use them for buying dollar equities. As I pointed out earlier, however, situations are liable to arise in which the acquisition of European dollar bonds with the aid of investment dollars might become worth while.

As we shall see later, there are in London markets in investment currencies other than investment dollars, but since they are unimportant compared with the investment dollars and in any case their rates are based entirely on that of the investment dollar, we propose to confine our analysis largely to the latter.

Markets in investment currencies arise from partial exchange controls under which capital transfers are restricted. The investment dollar market applies to them the principle of bilateralism under which there can be no net export of capital because additional foreign securities can only be acquired out of the proceeds of realised foreign securities. U.K. residents are only entitled to buy foreign securities if either they or some other U.K. holders of foreign securities had sold their holdings, so that investment dollars (or other investment currencies) are available, or can be purchased, to pay for the securities. This principle is applied in reverse to non-resident holdings of British securities. They can only be sold against payment in security sterling which can only be used for the purchase of other British securities. In actual practice there are exceptions to both rules but, broadly speaking, their operation aims at maintaining the *status quo* in respect of British portfolio investment abroad, which cannot be increased, and foreign portfolio investment in Britain, which cannot be reduced.

The system of investment dollars came into being in October 1947 when wartime exchange restrictions were relaxed and U.K. residents were authorised for the first time since the war to acquire new holdings of non-sterling securities, as distinct from turning over their existing foreign portfolio investments. Until then U.K. residents were only allowed to buy foreign securities if they sold their existing holding of foreign securities, the exact proceeds of which had to be reinvested immediately. Under the new regulations U.K. investors were entitled to reinvest abroad the proceeds of foreign securities sold by themselves or by other U.K. holders. With the aid of these proceeds they are entitled to buy dollar securities from other U.K. residents or in foreign markets at any time within six months from the acquisition of investment dollars.

The British authorities have disinterested themselves in individual transactions so long as the total of foreign securities held by British residents are not increased. Banks and other firms authorised to act as depositaries for foreign securities have to report, nevertheless, each transaction to the Bank of England within two months.

Until May 1962 there were two categories of investment dollars. They were popularly called 'hard dollars' and 'soft dollars' according to whether they related to the purchase and sale of North American securities or of other foreign securities. Since this system is no longer in operation there is no need to investigate it. Today investment dollars — variously called also 'security dollars', 'premium dollars' or 'switch dollars' — can be used for the acquisition of any eligible non-sterling security quoted on a recognised Stock Exchange.

The same rules that apply to investment dollars also apply to the foreign currency proceeds of other non-sterling securities. Thus the proceeds of German securities constitute investment marks which can be retained for six months and can be used for buying other German securities, or converted into investment dollars or other investment currencies, either for the purpose of immediate purchase of any foreign securities, or for keeping them for future requirements. The proceeds of Swiss securities constitute investment Swiss francs, the proceeds of Dutch securities investment guilders, etc. Because they are interchangeable with the investment dollar their quotation cannot deviate from that of the latter.

From time to time, increased activity in some investment currency develops. For instance, during the late 'fifties there was an active market in Canadian investment dollars and more recently in investment D. marks and investment lire, and even more recently in investment pesetas. But it is only the market in U.S. dollars that is always active, though its turnover has its ups and downs. Since investment currencies are now interchangeable, very often investment dollars are used for the purchase of the securities of countries such as Canada, Japan, Portugal, the Scandinavian countries, etc., whose investment currencies are not easily obtainable as a rule, unless the buyer bids up the premium to a sufficient level to induce holders of securities to realise their holdings and dispose of the proceeds. There would be no object in doing so, since investment dollars are always available at the current market price.

There is an official quotation of the premium on the investment dollars every day on the London Stock Exchange. It is based on the current sterling-dollar exchange rate of the day. Dealers, on the other hand, base their premium on the sterling-dollar parity of $2·80. This discrepancy often gives rise to irritating misunderstandings.

Investment dollars and other investment currencies have a peculiar market that differs materially from the markets in ordinary foreign exchanges. To a large but varying extent dealings in them are transacted outside the foreign exchange market, between stock departments of banks and Stock Exchange firms specialising in dollar securities. Foreign exchange dealers had successfully resisted the claims of money market departments to deal in Euro-dollars, because Euro-dollar transactions are closely related to foreign exchange transactions, and it is only right that they should be operated by the same people. On the same logic, however, their stock departments have a strong claim to handle investment dollars. Since it is they who handle transactions in dollar securities it is convenient if they handle also the investment dollar transactions arising from them. But owing to the increase in the proportion of transactions that are not related directly to security transactions, foreign exchange departments are taking a more active hand in the dealings of investment dollars.

Stockbrokers specialising in dollar securities and other foreign securities, London branches of American and other foreign brokers, etc., transact much business in investment dollars. In addition to all banks that are authorised dealers in foreign exchange, all stockbrokers and other firms who are authorised depositaries of foreign securities are entitled to deal in investment currencies.

The active market, however, consists of a small number of firms, some of which may conclude dozens of transactions on an active day while the large majority of the other firms may only conclude a few deals a week. Firms with a large turnover often have an opportunity to 'marry' buying or selling orders of their clients, in which case the transactions circumvent the market. Even foreign exchange departments sometimes transact business in investment dollars without the intermediary of foreign exchange brokers, because the commission — $\frac{1}{4}$ per cent for each party — tends to discourage them from employing brokers. In some foreign exchange departments a dealer or even several dealers specialise in investment dollars. To a large extent dealings take place independently of security transactions, for investment dollars and to a much less extent other investment currencies are often acquired and held by buyers who have no immediate intention — possibly no intention at all — to acquire dollar securities or other foreign securities.

Whether or not transactions take place within or outside the foreign exchange market, the technique of the market in investment dollars assumes increasingly the characteristics of ordinary foreign exchange business. Investment dollars can be bought and sold for forward as well as spot delivery.

In the absence of special arrangements, spot investment currencies are due to be delivered on the second clear business day after the conclusion of the deal, the practice being the same as in the foreign exchange market. But owing to the peculiar nature of business in investment currencies, whenever a transaction is connected with a security purchase the delivery of investment currencies is synchronised with the settlement of the security transaction. As the practice in respect of settlement varies according to the usage on various Stock Exchanges, the terms of delivery dates for spot transactions depend on the Stock Exchange on which the purchase of securities has to be settled. But the practice of delivery in two days is applied to the majority of the deals, partly because a high proportion of security transactions is concluded outside Stock Exchanges, and partly because a high proportion of investment currency transactions is not connected with security transactions. It is possible to arrange delivery on the same day or on the day following the conclusion of the deal.

There is a fair amount of forward dealing in investment dollars, and, to a much less extent, in other investment currencies. When a dealer sells investment dollars for forward delivery — whether to a client or in the market — he immediately covers the premium risk by buying spot investment dollars. As a result he has the use of the dollars until the forward contract matures. He may lend it in the Euro-dollar market, or he may carry out an ordinary swap transaction, selling spot dollars against forward dollars to be delivered when the forward contract in investment dollars matures. When a dealer buys forward investment dollars — whether from a client or in the market — he immediately sells spot investment dollars. He provides the spot dollars out of his holding of investment dollars, or borrows Euro-dollars, or carries out a swap transaction in ordinary dollars, buying spot dollars against forward dollars. The charge to the customer is usually based on the swap rates on ordinary dollars and on the premium on spot investment dollars.

Some firms are prepared to make two-way quotations of investment dollar rates, with a relatively narrow margin between their buying and selling rates. Possibly in the majority of instances they do so solely in order not to disclose their intention prematurely. If a firm quotes investment dollars at say, $11\frac{1}{4}$ to $11\frac{1}{2}$, it may only intend to buy at $11\frac{1}{4}$ and would back out of the deal if someone offered to buy from it at $11\frac{1}{2}$. Forward business in investment dollars is transacted fairly regularly up to three months but it is possible at times to deal for periods up to six months. There is often a very large turnover in forward investment dollars but hardly any in other investment currencies, though from time to time some investment currency becomes temporarily active because of some temporary special interest investors take in the securities of the country concerned.

In theory the maximum of the supply of investment dollars is represented by the total of quoted dollar securities held by private residents in the United Kingdom. According to the Radcliffe Report the size of this dollar 'pool' out of which the supply of investment dollars can be increased or replenished was estimated to be of the order of $4 billion in 1959 at market values prevailing in 1959. Giving evidence before the Radcliffe Committee on behalf of the Treasury, Sir Dennis Rickett admitted that this amount had tended to increase as a result of gaps in the exchange control. Through the free markets in certain parts of the Sterling Area such as the countries of the Persian Gulf or Hong Kong, additional dollar securities had been brought 'to inside the ring fence'. That gap was closed in July 1957, since when U.K. residents are no longer able to acquire foreign securities from other countries of the Sterling Area against payment in sterling. Even so, the control is not altogether watertight.

There is a variety of other channels through which the 'pool' could be increased legitimately. It could be increased by the receipt of legacies and gifts of securities from abroad. It could also increase — and has in fact increased considerably — through a rise in prices of dollar securities. Immigrants, too, can bring their securities with them. There can also be switches out of direct investments into portfolio investments, or out of unquoted foreign securities into eligible foreign securities.

There may be additions to the pool through the investment of certain foreign currency funds of a capital nature accrued to the residents of the U.K., such as capital proceeds of mortgages, real estates, mineral rights, life endowment policies, etc. Finally, on various occasions the Treasury disposed of Government-owned dollar securities through sales to U.K. residents.

There may be decreases in the 'pool' through export of securities by emigrants and repatriations by non-residents, also through gifts and legacies to non-residents or through straight-forward sales of investment dollars as ordinary dollars. The latter, however, is unlikely so long as there is a premium on investment dollars, because sellers would lose the premium. It did occur during periods when the premium declined to a negligible figure. The 'pool' must have been very low during the early post-war years, because most of the pre-war holdings had to be surrendered to the Treasury. Its amount must have increased very considerably during the 'fifties.

The officially endorsed idea that the total of private holdings of dollar securities constitute the potential supply of investment dollars is utterly fallacious and misleading. In the same sense, it would be justified to contend that, in the absence of exchange restrictions the total of bank deposits and note issues, amounting to some £25 billion, plus the Stock Exchange value of all sterling securities, would constitute the 'sterling pool' representing the maximum that could be made available to the foreign exchange market. In reality only a small fraction of the total is ever offered or is available for the requirements of the foreign exchange market. Similarly, only a fraction of the dollar securities and other foreign securities held by U.K. residents is ever likely to be made available at any given moment, or even over a period, to provide the counterpart of the demand for investment dollars. Most of these securities are firmly held by institutions or by private investors. While in theory it is conceivable that a very sharp rise in the premium might induce many of them to sell their securities for the sake of the profit on their investment dollars, in actual practice in most cases the premium would have to rise to such a high figure as to deter other investors from acquiring investment dollars.

There is, on the other hand, a certain amount of liquid investment dollars held either by investors who intend to re-invest their money sooner or later in dollar securities and are awaiting a favourable opportunity for it, or who simply like the feeling of holding dollar balances which give them the option of investing in sterling or non-sterling securities, or by professional dealers who choose to be long in investment dollars as a speculation on the increase of the premium. There are no estimates available about the total of such liquid dollars, but since returns are submitted to the authorities the latter must have an idea about it.

When the premium is at a high level, dealers are likely to keep down their holdings of investment dollars at a minimum, for fear that a contraction of the premium might inflict a loss on them. This is the reason why the premium is more sensitive when it is high. Comparatively small buying or selling orders are liable to move it quite disproportionately to the amount involved, because the counterpart is not readily available in the form of investment dollar balances held by dealers but must be produced by means of a stock transaction. It is not worth while to sell out dollar stock for the sake of providing a counterpart unless the premium rises to an attractive level.

In theory sellers of U.K. holdings of dollar securities have to reinvest the proceeds within six months as an alternative to selling them at a loss as ordinary dollars at the end of that period. In practice this restriction can be lawfully circumvented by the simple device of selling the investment dollars to a dealer on the understanding that the transaction would be reversed on the following day. Dealers are usually prepared to render this routine service to regular clients free of charge. At the end of another six months this formality can be repeated. The authorities are aware of this loophole but do not take any steps to stop it, nor even do they try to discourage it. So long as such transactions are reported to them by the dealers in their returns the authorities are able to keep track of these dollars, which is all that really matters to them. Indeed in many instances dealers simply report to the Bank of England the renewals of investment dollar holdings without going through the formalities of selling them and re-purchasing them.

The rules that govern the movements of the premium differ in many respects from those governing the fluctuations of ordinary exchange rates. Conventional foreign exchange theory is not always applicable to this market. While occasionally the premium on investment dollars moves in sympathy with spot dollars and forward dollars, more often than not it is largely, and at times completely, independent of them.

Let us now examine the influences affecting the movements

of the premium on investment currencies. In order to simplify the analysis we propose to confine ourselves to movements of investment dollars.

The following are the circumstances in which the premium on investment dollars tends to rise:

(1) If earnings on dollar equities or on dollar bonds are expected to rise.

(2) If Wall Street is firm or is expected to be firm for any other reason.

(3) If the dollar's prospects are viewed favourably.

(4) If U.K. residents holding in dollar securities who had safeguarded themselves against a fall in the premium on investment dollars no longer deem it necessary to maintain the hedge.

(5) If U.S. taxation on corporation profits or on interest on bonds is reduced or is expected to be reduced.

(6) If earnings on British equities or bonds fall or are expected to fall.

(7) If prices on the London Stock Exchange decline or are expected to decline for any other reasons.

(8) If sterling's prospects are regarded as unfavourable.

(9) If there is an increase in hedging against anti-capitalist measures in Britain.

(10) If certain British taxation is increased or is expected to be increased.

(11) If large amounts of new dollar issues are made or are expected to be made in Europe.

(12) If additional permits are issued, or are expected to be issued, for the use of investment dollars for direct investment abroad.

(13) If other kinds of demand for dollars are diverted into the investment dollar market by official measures.

(14) If exchange control relating to capital exports is tightened without, however, affecting the continued existence of the investment dollar system.

(15) If dealers' holdings of investment dollars are low.

(16) If the volume of capital available for investing in dollar securities is increased.

(17) If there is much call option dealing in dollar securities and if many buyers of options deem it necessary to cover by forward purchases of investment dollars.

(18) If for no matter what reason dealers and investors rightly or wrongly expect a widening of the premium.

Whenever dollar securities become more attractive to British residents the resulting demand tends to cause a rise in the premium on investment dollars. British holders are more reluctant to sell unless the sterling price of dollar securities or the premium on investment dollars rises to a level at which they become tempted to take their profits. We saw above that, if demand exceeds the supply held by dealers, would-be buyers have to bid up the premium in order to induce dealers to create additional investment dollars by selling dollar securities, or to induce investors to sell investment dollars they hold in readiness for future investment, or even to induce investors to sell securities in order to benefit by the high premium. An anticipation of an increase in the demand for dollar securities, whether because of favourable earnings prospects or of a cut, or even an expectation of a cut, of the U.S. tax on corporation profits, or for no matter what other reason, tends to put up the premium even before the actual pressure of additional demand for investment dollars becomes evident.

A similar effect is produced if the demand or anticipated demand for dollar securities is due not to an anticipation of their appreciation but to an anticipation of a fall in sterling securities, whether through a decline or anticipated decline in corporation earnings in Britain, or an increase in their taxation, or through no matter what other reason. Even if dollar securities do not become more attractive in an absolute sense, they become more attractive in a relative sense, which is sufficient reason for investors to acquire investment dollars.

Buyers and holders of dollar securities, having safeguarded themselves against the risk of a decline in the premium by selling investment dollars forward, may change their view about the prospects of the premium in which case they cover their short position and this causes an appreciation of investment dollars.

Another set of causes for a rise in the investment dollar premium is an increase in the volume of dollar securities in Europe. Only the types of securities which are considered to be worth buying in spite of the high premium tend to affect the premium. In existing circumstances dollar bond issues do not belong to this category, unless they assume the form of convertible debentures.

The Treasury's decision to grant permits for the use of investment dollars by industrial firms for direct investment abroad was mainly responsible for the sharp rise in the premium in recent years. Even an anticipation of the granting of additional permits to that end is sufficient to cause a rise. Rumours about alleged permits influence the premium from time to time. In the prolonged absence of any confirmation of such rumours it tends to drift back towards its previous level, but not necessarily to the full extent. The removal of a substantial amount of investment dollars for the requirements of direct investment reduces the supply of liquid investment dollars available, which is liable to produce a lasting effect on the premium even in the prolonged absence of further purchases for direct investment.

The diversion of some other categories of demand into the investment dollar market — for instance the decision in 1964 to grant permits to those wanting to buy real property abroad — tends to produce a similar effect.

The premium on investment dollars owes its very existence to the maintenance and efficient enforcement of exchange control on capital transactions. It would not have risen to well above 10 per cent in 1963–64 if U.K. residents found it comparatively easy and safe to circumvent exchange restrictions in preference to paying the high premium. British people are on the whole law-abiding, which means that the premium would have to rise to a relatively high level before even the less scrupulous amongst them yielded to the temptation of breaking the law instead of paying the premium. If new loopholes are discovered it tends to lower the premium until a level is reached at which it ceases to be considered worth while to break the law. On the other hand, a tightening of the control tends to bring the premium to a level at which the less scrupulous section of the financial community deems it worth while to risk evading the regulations — unless the accompanying increase in the risk of being found out deters them from yielding to the increased temptation.

But if the anticipated exchange control measures are such as to give rise to fears that sellers of investment dollars might be prevented from delivering the dollars sold, or if the possibility that the Government might order the surrender of privately-held dollar securities is envisaged, the effect is a decline in the demand for investment dollars and a decline of the premium. This is what actually happened towards the end of 1964.

The premium tends to rise whenever holdings of liquid investment dollars by dealers are at a low level. This depends not only on the actual amounts of their holdings but also on the way in which they have been temporarily invested. If they are unable to meet an increased demand out of their holdings they have to secure additional supplies in the ways described above, and it is only worth their while to do so if the premium rises sufficiently.

Whenever additional capital resources become available to the types of investors interested in acquiring dollar securities, and whenever some institutional change brings additional sets of investors into that category or increases the proportion of their resources available for investment in dollar securities, there is an increase in the demand for investment dollars.

While buyers of dollar securities may want to hedge against the investment dollar risk by selling investment dollars forward, those buying options on dollar securities may buy investment dollars forward in order to secure the exchange rate in case they should take up the option. They only do so if they anticipate a further widening of the premium, even though it would make it profitable for them to take up their option since it would cause a rise in the sterling price of the dollar securities. If they leave the investment dollars uncovered a fall in the premium would not affect their position, for a resulting fall in the sterling price of the securities is offset by a corresponding decline in the cost of acquiring the necessary investment dollars when the option matures.

If for no matter what reason an increase in the premium is anticipated, dealers want to increase their holdings of investment dollars for the sake of making a profit on their appreciation. Owing to the stability of most principal exchanges, the wide fluctuations in the premium attract a considerable volume of such speculative operations into the investment dollar market. The decision of investors whether to retain or realise the proceeds of their dollar securities and whether to cover in advance their anticipated future requirements of investment dollars, depends on the speculative views they take over the course of the premium.

The following is a summary of the effect produced by a rise in the premium:

(1) The sterling prices of dollar securities tend to rise in rough proportion to the rise in the premium.

(2) The resulting reduction in the sterling yield on dollar securities changes the differential between their yield and those of comparable dollar securities in favour of the former, thereby tending to divert demand to sterling securities.

(3) A high premium tends, therefore, to discourage demand for dollar securities, unless a further increase in the premium or in Wall Street is anticipated.

(4) An increase in the premium tends to stimulate realisations of dollar securities for the sake of profit-taking, unless a further rise in the premium or in Wall Street is anticipated.

(5) Although an increase in the premium has no direct bearing on the balance of payments, it tends to affect sterling unfavourably because it is regarded as an indication of a weakening confidence in sterling.

(6) As already pointed out, a wider premium tends to stimulate evasion of exchange control, by making it more profitable.

The ups and downs of the premium are even more perplexing than those of foreign exchange rates. On more than one occasion in recent years even experts were completely mystified by some unexpected declines of the premium. Such declines are liable to occur in the following circumstances:

(1) If U.S. corporation earnings fall, or are expected to fall.

(2) If dollar equities are expected to fall for any other reasons.

(3) If prospects of the dollar are believed to be unfavourable.

(4) If U.K. buyers or holders of dollar securities decide to cover the investment dollar risk by selling investment dollars forward.

(5) If U.S. corporation profits tax increases, or is expected to increase.

(6) If earnings on British equities increase, or are expected to increase.

(7) If the London Stock Exchange is expected to rise for any other reason.

(8) If sterling's prospects are viewed with optimism.

(9) If hedges previously arranged against the adoption of anti-capitalist measures are removed or reduced.

(10) If British taxation of corporation profits is reduced or is expected to be reduced.

(11) If the amount of new dollar bond issues in Europe declines.

(12) If no additional permits are issued for some time for direct investment or real property purchase abroad.

(13) If demand for portfolio investment is diverted or is expected to be diverted from the investment dollar market.

(14) If exchange control relating to capital export is relaxed or if it comes to be evaded more extensively.

(15) If a ban on dealings in investment dollars or the commandeering of dollar securities by the Government is anticipated.

(16) If dealers' holdings of liquid investment dollars are large.

(17) If capital available for investment in dollar securities declines.

(18) If for no matter what reason a fall in investment dollars is rightly or wrongly anticipated.

A diversion of demand for portfolio investment from the investment dollar market occurs when the authorities authorise certain investors or financial houses to pay for dollar securities with the aid of dollars borrowed in the United States, or with the aid of Euro-dollars. Occasionally even the temporary use of ordinary dollar holdings is permitted for approved portfolio investment, to avoid the development of a stringent situation.

It is necessary to deal with the paradoxical situation that is liable to arise when the premium is wide and is not expected to rise further. Although further demands for dollar securities means an additional demand for investment dollars by buyers, this demand does not cause the **premium** to widen, because its effect is offset by forward selling of investment dollars by the buyers of dollar securities who wish to hedge against a fall in the premium.

Although there is no justification for regarding the investment dollar premium as a barometer indicating the extent of an overvaluation of sterling, to some extent the premium does express in certain circumstances market opinion on the prospects of the sterling-dollar rate. On various occasions when sterling came under a cloud during the post-war period the premium was inclined to widen. This was because to some extent investment dollars or dollar securities bought with the aid of investment dollars were used as a hedge against devaluation. But on other occasions pressure on sterling was not accompanied by a widening of the premium on investment dollars.

The experience of 1949 conclusively provided that the use of investment dollars, or even the purchase of dollar securities bought with the aid of investment dollars, as a hedge against devaluation was utterly ill-advised. On the eve of the devaluation of sterling the premium on investment dollars was 36 per cent, and immediately after the devaluation it went down to 4 per cent. Considering that the extent of the devaluation was $30\frac{1}{2}$ per cent, those who bought investment dollars as a hedge on the eve of the devaluation lost on the fall of the premium more than they gained on the rise in the sterling-dollar rate. Although the extent to which the prices of individual dollar securities was affected by the devaluation varied widely, in the majority of instances the rise in their sterling price did not fully compensate holders for the fall in the premium. That is to say, if they sold out immediately after the devaluation they suffered a loss, but if they waited a little longer the premium rose once more and soon reached a level at which they were able to make a profit. Even so, the experience of September 1949 goes to show that an insurance premium against devaluation, in the form of the investment dollar premium that represents the market's expectation of the full extent of an impending devaluation, is apt to prove grossly excessive. For one thing, it is seldom possible to be certain about the imminence of a devaluation until it is officially announced, and in any case it is not easy to guess the extent of the impending devaluation.

Needless to say, it is much cheaper to insure against devaluation by means of forward exchange operations. During the first half of 1964 the covering of exchange risk by means of a forward exchange transaction costs a fraction of 1 per cent, while the premium on investment dollars has been fluctuating between 10 and 14 per cent. The difference is even more striking than would appear from their figures if we remember that for brief periods the actual cost of forward cover is a bare fraction of its percentage per annum, while the cost of covering by means of purchasing investment dollars is the same for a day as for a year. But U.K. residents are only permitted to take advantage of forward exchange facilities if they are engaged in foreign trade or in other approved international transactions. Otherwise the only legitimate channel through which they could attempt to hedge is through the investment dollar market, which is too costly a way of hedging and is apt to defeat the object.

If only this fact were realised by most of those concerned, the extent to which the premium is determined by the views taken of sterling-dollar rates prospects would be negligible. But in spite of the experience of 1949 there are many U.K. residents who are inclined to regard investment dollars as a suitable hedge against sterling devaluation. This view, however mistaken it may be, is liable to affect the premium to some extent, even though the rational behaviour of most of those concerned will prevent a recurrence of the experience of 1949.

Political prospects are a much more important factor in determining the premium. During 1963–64 the high level of the premium was largely due to fears of a Socialist victory at the approaching general election, which induced many investors to prefer dollar securities to sterling securities. The premium declined below 10 per cent when in August 1964 Conservative prospects appeared to improve. Later the premium widened once more, but, contrary to expectations, the Labour Party's victory was not followed by a spectacular widening of the premium. It actually narrowed considerably, because fears of a ban on dealings and of a commandeering of dollar securities discouraged demand. This influence more than offset the effects of hedging against anti-capitalist measures and of higher taxation.

War scares tend to cause a widening of the premium on investment dollars because, although modern wars are likely to be world-wide, it is assumed by many European investors that their money would be safer if invested across the Atlantic.

We already pointed out that in Holland and Belgium the monetary authorities have intervened systematically over a period of years in order to keep the premium on reinvestment dollars and finance account dollars respectively at a fraction of 1 per cent. They are under no obligation to do so and may at any time wish to discontinue their intervention if heavy purchases of securities by Dutch or Belgian residents should ever threaten to deplete their gold reserves. In Britain, on the other hand, the authorities usually abstain from supporting the market for investment dollars. On the contrary, from time to time they adjust the exchange regulations in the sense of permitting the use of investment dollars for purposes other than for which they had originally been created. There were, however, some indications of official support in October 1964, attributed to the Government's desire to prevent a spectacular widening of the premium in connection with the general election.

Since 1962 it has become possible to obtain license for direct investment abroad in cases in which the authorities would refuse license for the purchase of foreign exchange in the ordinary market. In 1964 buyers of real property abroad were permitted to use the investment dollar market. Any such additional demand necessarily increases the premium and the authorities have been subjected to much criticism for their policy. Possibly it may be explained on the ground of wanting to discourage demand for foreign securities, though, considering that the bilateralist principle is applied to such transactions, there does not seem to be any point in artificially widening the premium for that purpose. On the other hand, the critics are on sound ground when pointing out that a widening of the premium encourages evasion of exchange control resulting in an export of capital — which is precisely what the system aims at preventing. They are also right in contending that it produces an unfavourable psychological effect liable to affect sterling adversely. An argument in favour of the official policy is that the Government prefers direct investment to portfolio investment and wishes to increase the latter without adding to the burden of the balance of payment, even at the cost of penalising portfolio investment.

A possible explanation is that the authorities have become misled by their own estimate of the size of the 'dollar pool'. On the assumption that $4 billion or more are available; it may seem reasonable to allot a few hundred millions to meet requirements of direct investment — though even on that assumption it seems absurd for the authorities to encourage British people to establish permanent residence abroad and thus to avoid British taxation, by making it easier to finance the purchase of real property abroad. If only the authorities realised that their estimate of the size of the dollar pool is for practical purposes meaningless because most of the dollar securities are not available for investment dollars, and that the amount involved in licenses for direct investment and real property purchase must be compared with the estimated supplies of liquid investment dollars, not with their theoretical potential total, they might have been less generous in granting licenses for such purposes.

Possibly it was the somewhat delayed realisation of the fact that induced the authorities in 1964 to offset the additional buying pressure on investment dollars by granting licenses to U.K. residents for buying dollar securities with the aid of borrowed dollars. If so, both investors making use of this concession and the authorities based their attitude on the dubious assumption that pressure of demand for investment dollars was likely to decline by the time the dollar credits or Euro-dollar deposits used for financing the purchase matured.

We saw above that holding investment dollars is far from being an ideal way of hedging against a devaluation of sterling. On the other hand, many dealers acquire and hold them to speculate on a further rise of the premium itself, regardless of their view on sterling. We already observed that at a time when the fluctuations of the spot rate are limited by the support points under the Bretton Woods system of stable exchange rates, and when even forward rates fluctuate usually within narrow limits, the investment dollar market provides a better scope for making profits on speculative operations.

In an article in the *Economic Journal* of 1950, Margaret Rix put forward a theory according to which the premium on investment dollars is due to some extent on what she calls convertibility-preference. While a U.K. resident holder of sterling can only invest it in sterling securities a U.K. resident holding investment dollars has the choice between investing it in dollar securities or selling his holding and investing the proceeds in sterling securities. She rightly points out that a holding of investment dollars is much less useful than a holding of ordinary dollars. 'It is, however, the next best thing that British residents can hold for any length of time.' Holders of investment dollars are in a position to switch in and out of British and American securities. In respect of the relative attractiveness of sterling and dollar securities Margaret Rix points out that a British holder does not regard the relative merits of different American securities in quite the same way as Wall Street. Difference in yields of comparable British and U.S. securities are liable to affect only specific shares. Nevertheless, the dollar premium is uniform because to holders of investment dollars U.S. securities are freely interchangeable and one investment dollar is regarded as useful as another in the same way that to a retailer of goods a pound note is as good as any other pound note.

CHAPTER 13

SOME BROADER IMPLICATIONS

WE have already examined several of the broader implications of dollar issues in Europe in the chapters on their impact on domestic interest rates, international interest rates, exchange rates and Euro-dollars. Some of these implications call, however, for further considerations, and there are, moreover, additional broader aspects to be considered. To some of them passing reference has already been made but which deserve further attention. The following is a selection of these points, to be covered in the present chapter:

(1) European dollar bond issues, by mobilising dormant dollar holdings, contribute towards the increase of international liquidity.

(2) They consolidate fluid dollar balances, thereby contributing towards international stability.

(3) In normal conditions they offset adverse balances of payments on current account and neutralise the effect of disequilibrating short-term capital movements.

(4) In abnormal conditions they accentuate the disequilibrium in the balance of payments.

(5) They diffuse capital issuing activity that has been centred too one-sidedly in New York since the war.

(6) They contribute towards a more even international allocation of capital resources.

(7) They contribute towards an integration of the European capital markets.

(8) They further the trend towards an internationalisation of finance.

(9) They strengthen the dollar's rôle as an international currency by providing it with an important additional international function.

(10) They provide a channel between long-term and short-term interest rates.

(11) They create a set of international long-term interest rates towards which local long-term interest rates tend to adjust themselves.

(12) They create a capital issuing mechanism which can be placed in the service of domestic as well as foreign issues.

One of the many unanswered and possibly unanswerable questions raised by the system of European dollar bond issues is whether they tend on balance to mobilise dormant dollar balances or to consolidate fluid balances. In other words, whether they tend to increase or reduce the velocity of circulation of foreign-owned dollar balances. Evidently the system produces effects in both senses, so that the only question we have to answer is, which of its two conflicting effects outweighs the other. The answer depends on the nature of the dollars used for subscribing to the loans and also on the intentions of their old owners and of their new owners. This subject has already been touched upon in Chapters 8 and 9 when dealing with the impact of dollar bond issues on Euro-dollars and on the dollar exchange. Owing to its importance it is necessary, however, to examine it more closely. In doing so we must guard ourselves against allowing our conclusions to be influenced by any prejudice for or against international expansion — whether, in our opinion, an increase of international liquidity is a Good Thing or a Bad Thing.

The issue of European dollar bonds tends to convert dormant foreign-owned dollars into active foreign-owned dollars in the following circumstances:

(1) If long-term time deposits or other dormant non-resident balances in the United States, or long-term Euro-dollar deposits, are employed for financing the transactions.

(2) If proceeds of non-residents' dollar investments sold to U.S. residents are used for that purpose.

(3) If the borrower spends the formerly dormant dollars on additional imports.

(4) If the borrower sells formerly dormant dollars in the

foreign exchange market and the buyer spends them on additional imports or maintains them in a liquid form.

(5) If the borrower sells formerly dormant dollars to his monetary authorities and the latter spend them on Government expenditure abroad or sell them in support of the local currency, or use them as a basis of domestic credit expansion.

Issues of European dollar bonds tend to consolidate fluid foreign dollar assets in the following circumstances:

(1) If sight deposits or short-term foreign deposits in the U.S., or sight or short-term Euro-dollar deposits or short-term credits are used for financing the investment in dollar bonds.

(2) If subscribers buy dollars formerly held in a liquid form.

(3) If the borrower uses the dollar proceeds for the repayment of short-term dollar debts.

(4) If the borrower uses the dollar proceeds to obviate the need for short-term borrowing of dollars.

(5) If the dollars bought from the borrower by his monetary authorities are retained by the latter in the form of dollar reserve without expanding credit, or if they are withdrawn in the form of gold.

Any loosening of dormant dollars furthers the cause of expansion but weakens the cause of stability. Any consolidation of fluid dollars is an advantage from the point of view of stability but a disadvantage from the point of view of expansion. However, to answer the broad question whether a loosening of consolidation in general is on balance an advantage or a disadvantage is outside the scope of this book. Our present task is confined to trying to ascertain in which direction the system tends to operate in various conceivable circumstances, without trying to suggest an answer whether its operation is for good or for evil from that point of view. There can be no categorical answer to our question. It depends on a multitude of circumstances. But our tentative answer is that in the majority of instances it tends to consolidate and stabilise.

Another major question is whether the system tends to balance or unbalance the balance of payments. It is understood of course that technically the balance of payments must always balance. What matters is the way in which it balances, in which sense unilateral buying or selling pressure on the exchange through a surplus or a deficit tends to cause exchange movements in order to set in motion the market mechanism to attract counterparts in the form of balancing or disturbing short-term fund movements.

While opinion must be divided about the relative advantages and disadvantages of an increase or reduction of the proportion of fluid and consolidated dollar holdings, there is no room for two opinions on the advantages of equilibrium in the balance of payments — in the sense in which it is achieved without unwanted short-term movements of funds or other unwanted changes in the balance of international indebtedness — even if there is room for disagreement on its place in one's list of priorities.

It is true, a too rigid application of the principle that it is an absolute advantage to keep international accounts in permanent equilibrium would mean a rigid maintenance of the *status quo* in respect of the international distribution of monetary gold reserves. Surpluses and deficits are sometimes necessary in order to bring about a more convenient redistribution of monetary gold. Broadly speaking, however, it remains true that in the interest of international stability it is an advantage if long-term capital movements tend to offset surpluses and deficits on the current balance of payments and on the balance of international movements of short-term funds.

Dollar bond issues in Europe tend to be equilibrating in the following ways:

(1) By diverting borrowing by financially strong countries from New York to their own capital markets.

(2) By diverting borrowing by financially weak countries from New York to financially strong European countries with export surpluses available for the purpose.

(3) By mopping up floating dollars that are liable to cause disequilibrating movements of short-term funds through speculative selling, movement of flight money or arbitrage.

(4) By consolidating foreign short-term debts owed to the United States.

(5) By enabling financially weak countries to borrow more than they could have in New York alone.

(6) By strengthening the gold and dollar reserves of financially weak countries.

European dollar bond issues have a disequilibrating effect on the balance of payments in the following ways:

(1) By loosening dormant dollars, thereby increasing the chances of disturbing hot money movements.

(2) By adding to adverse pressure on sterling to the extent to which non-resident sterling balances are employed for financing the transactions.

(3) By enabling borrowing countries to pursue unsound monetary and economic policies instead of taking action to correct their balance of payments disequilibrium.

(4) By assisting the United States authorities to continue to maintain artificially low interest rates.

As in respect of 'fluidity *v.* consolidation', the operation of the system is liable to cut both ways also in respect of its effect on the balance of payments. In this respect, however, we are reasonably safe in concluding that by and large it operates in an equilibrating sense. It tends to reduce and even prevent the flagrantly disequilibrating process that was in operation until the middle of 1963, under which surplus countries such as France borrowed in New York in spite of their large export surpluses and in spite of the large adverse balance of the United States. But the issue of foreign bonds in Germany during 1964 in terms of D. marks did not contribute towards offsetting the affect of her export surplus, while mitigating the disequilibrating effect of the influx of foreign funds to Germany. The D. mark bond issues provided an opportunity for speculation on the chances of a D. mark revaluation without aggravating the international monetary disequilibrium and without causing domestic inflation in Germany. Speculators simply lent their money to the borrowing countries via Germany instead of lending it to Germany.

Another of the broader implications of the dollar bond issues is the rôle they play in the diffusion of capital issuing activities which had been centred too one-sidedly in New York until the middle of 1963. Perverted 'uphill' flows of capital, such as the flow from the United States to France referred to in the last paragraph, at a time when the adverse American balance and the favourable French balance called for a flow in the opposite sense, were largely due to the inadequacy of most European capital markets, especially that of Paris. This subject is covered in great detail in the Report of the United States Treasury on *Certain European Capital Markets* and we need not go into it in detail. The reason for the one-sided part played by New York in respect of foreign capital issues since the war lies in the fact that European financial centres with pre-war traditions for serving as international capital markets have been prevented, by a variety of circumstances, from resuming those functions after the war. Those circumstances were described in great detail in the United States Treasury's Report.

Although it had been for a long time an American ambition that New York should take London's place as the dominant financial centre of the world, the achievement of that ambition in the post-war era is now looked upon with mixed feelings in the United States. In more recent years American official circles, political circles and expert opinion have come to realise the grave responsibilities and disadvantages that a quasi-monopolistic position as the world's banker entails. The decision to adopt the Interest Equalisation Tax was the result of this change of attitude in favour of a diffusion of international capital issuing activities, change which came to be expressed by the publication of the United States Treasury's Report published with the declared object of assisting Europe in the development of rival capital markets that would divert business from New York.

A more even international allocation of capital resources is an undisputed advantage from the point of view of international economic progress. From this point of view dollar bond issues in Europe tend to perform the same service in respect of long-term capital as is performed by the Euro-dollar market in the sphere of short-term capital. So long as the perennial adverse balance of payments of the United States continues, the New York capital market is not in a position to meet in full the increased international demand on its resources for long-term capital without accentuating the gravity of the dollar problem. The spectacular increase of foreign long-term borrowing in New York during the first half of 1963 provided a warning which was wisely heeded by the Washington Administration.

Dollar bond issues in Europe tend to further the cause of a more even allocation of capital resources in the following ways:

(1) They take the place of the flow of funds from New York to countries in need of additional capital, at a time when the United States is anxious to reduce that flow.

(2) Conceivably European capital markets might even supply capital importing countries with capital in excess of the amount that would have been obtainable in New York even without reducing that flow.

(3) In some financial centres the dollar bond issues, by improving the capital issuing mechanism and by getting the investing public into the habit of subscribing to such issues, tend to encourage also a revival of local capital issuing activities.

(4) Dollar bond issues tend to modify the essentially local character of capital markets existing in some Continental countries.

The effect of dollar bond issues in Europe on the international distribution of capital is, however, necessarily limited in prevailing circumstances. The new issue markets do not cater for the requirements of developing countries which do not enjoy a sufficient degree of confidence to make it possible for them to borrow commercially on mutually acceptable terms, indeed on any terms at all. As things are, the market for dollar bonds is almost entirely for the benefit of relatively advanced countries.

Integration of European capital markets was one of the declared aims of the Rome Treaty. So far the progress in that direction has been confined to the sphere of direct investment within the Common Market. The barriers between the Six have remained virtually unchanged as far as issues of foreign bonds are concerned. Until 1963 foreign issuing activity consisted mainly of loans issued and placed largely in Germany, Switzerland, Holland and, to a less extent, Britain. It was not until the resumption of London's activity as a centre for issuing foreign loans that foreign loans came to be issued on a European scale and perceptible progress came to be made towards integration of European capital markets, not within the EEC but within the whole of Western Europe including Britain and Switzerland. Dollar issues were found more suitable for transactions of a truly international character than D. mark issues, Swiss franc issues, or even composite unit of account issues.

In an article in the June 1963 *Lloyds Bank Review*, Peter Kenen rightly points out that the weakness of European capital markets could only be remedied if those markets were consolidated. 'They would be more receptive to new issues if one could buy or sell a European bond on any European market.' In the post-war world none of the European markets is by itself in a position to serve as an alternative to the New York bond market. But an integration of the capital issuing facilities of all Western European markets would create a foreign bond market that would bear comparison with that of the United States. It would be idle to speculate what would have happened if Britain had joined the Common Market. But even without doing so, the co-operation of London's issuing houses with those of the Continent has in fact given rise to some degree of association between the leading non-American capital markets. It is true, there are still many bond issues made in Germany and Switzerland in which London banks take no direct part, and some essentially international loans were issued in 1963–64 by syndicates headed by Continental banks. But since the revival of foreign bond issuing activity in London a good many truly international loans have been issued by groups headed by London banks.

In my article in the June 1964 issue of *The National Banking Review*, published by the United States Treasury, in which I reviewed that Treasury's Report on *Certain European Capital Markets*, I expressed the opinion that the reason why the official American opinion is now in favour of a diffusion of international issuing activity was, in addition to a desire to relieve the

American balance of payments, to make more effective the application of the new monetary policy which aims at influencing long-term as well as short-term interest rates. I already pointed out that so long as New York was practically the only capital market in which countries in need of foreign capital could borrow on a large scale, any American policy decision to discourage such borrowing by means of raising long-term interest rates was doomed to remain largely ineffective. For countries in urgent need of foreign capital would always be willing to pay the higher interest rates, especially since those rates would be in any case lower than those prevailing in their domestic capital markets even if the required amounts were obtainable there.

This means that in the absence of alternative capital markets where long-term loans could be issued on terms comparable with those obtainable in New York, pressure on the dollar due to overlending abroad would continue in spite of higher long-term interest rates in New York, if adopted under the new post-Radcliffe monetary policy. The effects of that policy, aimed at mitigating the extent to which domestic short-term borrowers have to be penalised by shifting part of the burden from short-term borrowers on long-term borrowers, tends to be largely frustrated unless a diffusion of international capital issuing activity makes that policy more effective.

Whether the new monetary policy would necessarily be advantageous is open to doubt. If, as seems probable, it aims at maintaining interest rates in the United States at an artificially low level, its short-term advantages might have to be paid for dearly in the long run, in the form of depletion of gold reserve and increase of foreign short-term claims. What matters from the point of view with which we are here concerned is that, with the aid of efficient European markets to which unwanted foreign long-term loans can be diverted, the United States authorities are in a position to pursue more effectively the monetary policy of their choice.

The practice of issuing foreign dollar bonds in Europe has obviously contributed towards the progress of internationalisation of finance. Issuing centres have acquired the habit of lending in terms of the currency that serves best the purposes of the transactions instead of feeling bound to lending in terms of their own local currency. The existence of the new facilities make it easier for borrowers to raise capital in the cheapest market and in terms of a currency which suits their purpose. This effect again is the same in the sphere of long-term capital issuing activity as that of the Euro-dollar system in the sphere of international short-term credits. Lenders and borrowers feel no longer tied to transacting business solely in the lender's currency. Moreover, the foreign dollar bonds, like the Euro-dollar deposits, have a truly international market.

Internationalisation of finance is very far from being an unqualified advantage. An increase in the international character of financial markets means, in given circumstances, an increase in potential instability. The possibility of marketing the dollar bonds in several centres increases the possibility of hot money movements whenever the dollar comes under a cloud. But, then, anything that makes for a greater freedom in the international movements of funds — or, for that matter, of goods — tends to produce a similar potentially unsettling effect. There can be no safeguard against disturbing international movements of money except through exchange control. And even the advanced controls that existed in Britain in 1949 were unable to prevent a landslide against the pound leading to its devaluation.

International co-operation between issuing houses has long traditions. Centuries before loans came to be raised by means of the public issues practised in our days, transactions were often arranged with the participation of banking houses of more than one country. Before 1914, and again between the wars, international loans were often issued simultaneously in several markets. But on such occasions each issuing house usually operated in its own territory, and the issues were divided into separate local tranches for that purpose. The recently issued dollar loans, and also the unit of account loans, on the other hand, were handled by members of international banking groups without regard to national frontiers. In particular London's share, since it could not be placed in Britain, had to be placed with overseas clients — amongst them investors resident in countries whose banks were participating in the consortium. To try to place the bonds in another country which is represented on the consortium is no longer considered poaching on other issuing houses' preserves. Underwriting of such issues has also become more international in character.

The issue of dollar bonds by international groups of European banks and the arrangement of dealing facilities on several European Stock Exchanges constitutes an important step in the direction of international co-operation aiming at a better satisfaction of capital requirements.

It would be idle to deny the fact that the dollar has to a large extent replaced the pound as the world currency. Most Central Banks outside the Sterling Area now hold most of their foreign exchange reserves in dollars. Most refugee funds have gravitated towards New York during the post-war era and they are still held in dollars with American banks, even if much of the foreign-owned dollars are re-deposited through the Euro-dollar markets. Much of foreign trade outside that of countries of the Sterling Area is now conducted in dollars rather than in sterling. The Euro-dollar system has given the dollar added significance as an international currency, even though the same system of transactions in foreign currency deposits is applied in smaller degrees to sterling and other major currencies. Now the use of the dollar as the currency unit of loans issued for non-American borrowers by non-American banks outside the United States, and taken up by investors outside the United States, has created an additional use for dollars, and this tends to create an additional demand for dollars in the international field.

One of the major defects of the modern monetary system, denounced by the Radcliffe Report and other authoritative voices, is the absence of adequate channels of communication between short-term credits and long-term loans. There can be no time-arbitrage between them. The market in European dollar bonds provides a possibility — it would be unduly optimistic to put it higher than that at the time of writing — for the development of such channels. As and when maturities of Euro-dollar deposits become longer it will become easier to switch into European dollar bonds and vice versa. It is true, the two forms of investment are not strictly comparable. Their security is not identical, and funds invested in dollar bonds can be realised without awaiting their maturity, though holders may have to accept a loss. But this difference in liquidity may be overcome by an escape clause that can be inserted in time deposit arrangements.

We discussed in Chapter 7 the structure of international long-term interest rates created by the European dollar bond market. Should this market expand that structure might well influence domestic long-term interest rates which would tend to gravitate towards it. In countries which do not possess a good market in long-term bonds long-term interest rates are apt to be too high in spite of the relatively low short-term interest rates. The existence of a rival market might affect the whole structure of domestic long-term interest rates.

A really extensive popularisation of European dollar bonds might induce even financially strong countries to use that market for domestic borrowing, not because the local currency is distrusted by local investors but because interest rates would be lower owing to the international marketability of the bonds. Some Governments of advanced countries, such as Denmark and Norway, have already discarded inhibitions which would have prevented them until recently from issuing their loans in terms of dollars in the domestic market. So long as part of the loans are issued in foreign centres, even though the bulk of it is issued in the local market, they do not feel the transaction is detrimental to the prestige of the national currency.

Thanks to the practice of European dollar bond issues, there has been a strong revival of foreign lending. Before the Wall Street slump the issue of bonds was the main form in which long-term capital was lent abroad, but during the 1930s, the war and the early post-war period it had fallen virtually into disuse. Its place was taken partly by inter-Government loans and partly by direct investment. The former has grave disadvantages as it deprives borrowers of the incentive to achieve creditworthiness. The latter is confined to large industrial firms and provides no facilities for institutional or private investors. The issue of dollar bonds — or, for that matter, unit of account bonds — is the right approach and should go a long way towards assisting in the process of non-official investment abroad which is based much more broadly than direct investment, both from the point of view of the origin of the funds and their destination.

The advantages of the development of a European market for dollar bonds and bonds in denomination of other currency units may be summarised as follows:

(1) Advantages to issuing houses and underwriters.
    (*a*) Earning of commission.
    (*b*) Capital gains (if any).
    (*c*) Gaining experience.
    (*d*) Gaining additional prestige.
    (*e*) Securing additional foreign clients.
    (*f*) Earnings by paying agents for the loans.

(2) Advantages to investors.
    (*a*) Higher yields than dollar bonds issued in New York.
    (*b*) Additional facilities to spread their risk.
    (*c*) Additional facilities to hedge against a devaluation of their currency.

(3) Advantages to borrowing countries.
    (*a*) Meeting balance of payments deficit.
    (*b*) Stimulating growth of the economy.
    (*c*) Strengthening the gold and foreign exchange reserve.
    (*d*) Relieving scarcity of credit.
    (*e*) Meeting budgetary deficit.
    (*f*) Consolidating floating debts.

(4) Advantages to lending country.
    (*a*) Neutralising unwanted balance of payments surplus.
    (*b*) Stimulating exports.
    (*c*) Earning invisible exports (commissions, etc.).
    (*d*) Securing economic influence in borrowing country.
    (*e*) Supporting allied and friendly countries.
    (*f*) Developing technique which is liable to assist in domestic capital issues.

(5) Advantages to entrepôt countries.
    (*a*) Earning invisible exports.

(*b*) Keeping lending mechanism in practice.

(*c*) Strengthening valuable international connections.

(*d*) Gaining prestige.

(*e*) Stimulating exports.

(*f*) Supporting friendly countries.

There are, admittedly, many items on the other side of the balance sheet. The practice entails disadvantages and risks. But in view of its many advantages there can be little doubt that its adoption has been a welcome step in the right direction.

CHAPTER 14

THE FUTURE OF EUROPEAN DOLLAR LOANS

When I was writing my book on *The Euro-Dollar System* in 1963 I had no hesitation to conclude that the Euro-dollar market had come to stay and that, temporary fluctuations apart, it would continue to expand. Although my conclusion about the future of European dollar bond issues is on balance similar, I do not feel justified in being quite so categorical in asserting it as I was in respect of the Euro-dollar market. The latter had a fundamental justification in that it resulted in a segregation of wholesale banking from retail banking, enabling those who transacted in large amounts to pay lower interest rates and to receive higher deposit rates than the multitude of small customers whose accounts involve much more clerical labour for the same totals. There is no comparable fundamental justification for the new device of European dollar bond issues, the development of which is the result of practical expediency which might conceivably prove to be temporary.

Nevertheless, on balance, it seems probable that the new device, like the device of Euro-dollar deposits, has come to stay even if its use were to suffer temporary eclipse from time to time. This conclusion rests on the following arguments:

(1) The United States is unlikely ever to assume again so unilaterally the burden of satisfying the capital requirements of the five continents as she did until the late 'fifties. Whatever form the official policy aiming at preventing the recurrence of that state of affairs will assume — it need not necessarily assume the form of perpetuating the Interest Equalisation Tax — it is likely to try to divert from New York to Western European capital markets much of the foreign demand for capital. The effect of the Interest Equalisation Tax on foreign borrowing in New York is incalculable and it is possible that in a number of instances it will not prevent the issue of foreign bonds in the

United States. Even so, it is bound to divert to Europe a
number of issues, and in any case the demand for long-term
capital is so heavy that a resumption of foreign borrowing in
New York need not mean a cessation of foreign borrowing in
Europe in the form of dollar bond issues.

Even if the United States balance of payments should
achieve once more a steady surplus, the lesson taught by the
experience of the late 'fifties and early 'sixties is bound to be
remembered in Washington. Those responsible for shaping
long-term monetary policy are likely to have sufficient foresight
to continue to aim at encouraging the maintenance of efficient
capital markets in Europe by discouraging unlimited foreign
long-term borrowing in New York. Moreover, it would take a
long series of export surpluses to raise the American gold reserve
to the desired high level. Not until the United States possesses once more an impressive surplus of gold reserves over
foreign short-term dollar claims will it appear once more expedi-
ent to encourage unlimited foreign long-term borrowing in New
York.

(2) Until the autumn of 1964 it was widely believed that
the actual application of the Interest Equalisation tax, by re-
moving the uncertainty created by its anticipation, would lead
to a resumption of foreign borrowing in New York and would
mean the end of the European issues of foreign dollar bonds.
Up to the end of 1964 such expectations received no confirmation, even though there was some foreign long-term borrowing
in New York following on the actual application of the new
tax in August 1964. The flow of dollar bond issues in London
continued during the autumn unabated.

(3) The facilities of the European capital markets are likely
to improve. Fiscal and exchange control handicaps are likely
to be reduced in the long run, even if relapses cannot be ruled
out. As far as London is concerned, the Labour Government
does not appear to wish to discourage foreign lending in its rôle
of an entrepôt for foreign capital. In the long run it does not
seem unreasonable to hope that the exchange restrictions which
at present prevent active participation of British investors in
dollar bond issues might be relaxed, or, what is much more

likely, the premium on investment dollars which deters British residents from subscribing will cease to be prohibitive. Among the Continental capital markets France and Germany are certain to pursue policies to encourage their expansion both from the point of view of their interest in preventing imported inflation and from that of their international prestige. Already Germany has made good progress in 1964, especially in the issue of foreign D. mark bonds. A prolonged period of stability would enable the investing public in both countries to overcome their aversion to foreign bond issues based on their disastrous experience in the not too distant past.

(4) There can be no certainty about the permanency of the use of the dollar as the main currency in which international loans will continue to be issued in Europe. At the time of writing the dollar appears to be the most suitable currency for that purpose because, after a series of dollar scares, it has come to be trusted once more, and because there appears to be no likelihood for any early change in its gold parity. So long as lenders are satisfied that the dollar is not likely to be devalued, and so long as borrowers feel they need not fear its revaluation, the dollar will constitute the compromise on whose choice the conflicting interests of the two parties can meet.

But there have been too many fundamental changes in the trends of, and outlook for, every major currency in my lifetime to feel justified in expressing a firm opinion whether or not the dollar is likely to remain in its present position as the near-ideal currency of foreign bond issues. There is always a possibility that dollar scares might revive. Alternatively, a return of acute dollar scarcity might revive anticipations of its revaluation. In either case borrowers or lenders would have to find an alternative currency unit for foreign bond issues.

Conceivably some other currency might assume for a time the same position which the dollar occupies at present. At the time of writing the D. mark is being used extensively as the currency of foreign bond issues, but mainly in Germany. Conceivably there may be a revival of financial nationalism, and for considerations of prestige each country participating in international loans might come to insist that their tranche should

be issued in their respective national currencies. All this is in
the realm of conjecture. It is possible that persistent anticipation of a revaluation of the D. mark or some other hard currency
might induce foreign investors to accept a very low yield on
bonds expressed in such currencies for the sake of the prospects
of revaluation profits, and that debtors might yield to the temptation of risking a revaluation loss for the certain benefit of
borrowing at a low cost. In that case the currency in question
might well replace the dollar, at least temporarily, as the
currency of European foreign bond issues. In actual fact,
during 1964 a number of not altogether first-rate borrowers
were willing to borrow in D. marks in London in spite of the
revaluation risk involved.

(5) It is possible that, apart altogether from any ups and
downs in the relative position of the dollar and of other hard
currencies, the formula embodied in bond issues in terms of
composite unit of account might find wider application if and
when the public should grow used to its complications. There
is a great deal to be said for such an international currency unit.
Many debtors and creditors might conceivably come to the
conclusion sooner or later that it would be more than worth
their while to forgo their chances of benefiting by a change in
parities in their favour, for the sake of being safeguarded
against losses arising from changes in parities to their detriment.
The main obstacle to a popularisation of units of accounts loans
lies in the highly involved and obscure character of the formula
on which they are based, and some degree of uncertainty about
the legal position until it has been tested by law court decisions.
This obstacle is by no means insurmountable and the possibility
that in the course of time unit of account loans might overshadow
in importance dollar loans and all other types of foreign loans
cannot be ruled out. Such a change would take time, however,
for at present a large proportion even of sophisticated institutional investors are still uncertain about the value of the safeguards offered by the composite unit of account formula.
Indeed at the time of writing the popularity of the device seems
to be declining rather than increasing.

We must also consider the remote possibility that sooner or

later the United States Government might follow the Swiss example in objecting to the use of the dollar as the currency unit for loans issued abroad. As I pointed out earlier, however, the position of the United States with her vast domestic bond market is totally different from that of Switzerland whose relatively narrow bond market is liable to be affected by the issue of loans outside Switzerland in terms of Swiss francs. The only argument that could possibly be put forward in favour of American policy objecting to such use of the dollar — if we rule out the possibility of the United States adopting exchange control — is that European dollar bonds offer investment facilities for American capital that has found its way abroad for the purpose of fiscal evasions. Since, however, there are many alternative investment facilities for such capital that argument is hardly likely to be conclusive.

(6) A spectacular recovery of Britain's economic position might restore sterling to its previous rôle as the leading international currency as a result of a complete elimination of all exchange control and the accumulation of an impressive gold reserve fed by perennial balance of payments surpluses. Although there is no harm in dreaming about this it would be wishful thinking to regard it as a distinct possibility. It seems probable that in Britain exchange restrictions on capital transactions have come to stay, even if there is a remote possibility of their mitigation. Before Britain can hope to achieve and maintain a really satisfactory balance of payments position and reserve position her trade unions would have to be cured of what has come to be known all over the world as 'the English disease'. Unfortunately, miracles seldom happen in the 20th century. There is, on the other hand, a possibility that workers in all industrial countries might catch the English disease, in which case Britain would cease to be handicapped by it.

(7) A setback in international capital issuing activity might occur as a result of some international financial crisis. Wholesale defaults by foreign debtors, or a currency chaos comparable to that of the 'thirties would effectively discourage the issue of dollar bonds, as indeed any form of foreign lending, as it did in the 'thirties. Such a setback would be temporary, however,

even if it might be of a long duration. Having become familiar with the device of issuing loans in terms of a foreign currency unit, the capital markets would revert to its use, as it would undoubtedly revert to the use of Euro-dollar deposits, as soon as conditions made it possible.

(8) It is possible that the Labour Government will adopt exchange control which would prevent the issue of dollar bonds in London. This would constitute a setback to the international distribution of capital resources. Even though Western European capital markets would continue to operate, in the absence of London's participation their integration into a market big enough to serve as an alternative to New York would become more difficult. But sooner or later Britain is likely to discard economic isolationism and London would be allowed to resume its present rôle as an entrepôt for foreign capital.

Taking everything into consideration it seems probable, though not absolutely certain, that the system of dollar loan has come to stay and that, temporary ups and downs apart, its application will expand with the expansion of European capital markets. It is possible to envisage the development of really active European dollar bond markets with a large turnover both within each market and between them. A basic condition for such an expansion would be, however, a restoration of confidence in fixed interest-bearing securities in general. Should creeping inflation proceed unhindered and at an accelerating pace, distrust in the maintenance of the purchasing power of the dollar, as that of other currencies, is bound to increase. A growing inflation-consciousness of investors would necessitate the payment of increasingly high interest rates on foreign loans as on domestic loans. Alternatively the issue of dollar bonds for private borrowers might increasingly assume the form of convertible debentures whose equity-content would overcome distrust in the stability of the monetary unit. Indeed the possibility that bond issues might be replaced to a large but increasing extent by equity issues cannot be ruled out. On the other hand, it is conceivable that Governments might issue bonds on which the payment of interest and principal would rise with the cost of living or some other index. No such bonds have been issued abroad so far, but it is a distinct possibility.

However this may be, the formula of European dollar bond issues is fulfilling at the time of writing, and is likely to continue to fulfil, for some time at any rate, a highly important constructive rôle. It has contributed and is likely to continue to contribute towards the expansion of European capital markets in accordance with the basic interests of progress. Its survival and expansion could and should be greatly assisted by improvements aiming at encouraging international lending.

One of such improvements, which is actually in force in the United States and in Germany, is the insurance of foreign investments by the Government against political risk. A liberal definition of the meaning of political risk would greatly encourage long-term lending to countries which need it the most. It is a preferable alternative to continued Government aid in the form of inter-Government loans, because of popular conception, based on experience, that default on debts owed to foreign Governments, or even their outright repudiation, is judged by standards that are fundamentally different from those applied to similar acts committed against private creditors. Even some of the most important Governments repudiated War Debts after the first World War, and after the second World War such debts were virtually wiped out by agreement between the creditors and most debtors.

The worst that can happen to foreign investments guaranteed by the Government of the lending country is that the taxpayer would have to shoulder the burden eventually. If such loans are issued in place of outright gifts or loans by Governments that are defaulted upon eventually the taxpayer would be no worse off, and he even stands a chance that some of the guaranteed debts might not be defaulted upon.

But even Government guarantees are open to objection on the same grounds, though to a less extent, as inter-Government loans, *i.e.*, that the debtor might regard them as semi-political debts which could be defaulted upon as a matter of course. In any case, such guarantees obviate the necessity for borrowers to become creditworthy by building up a reputation for integrity.

The correct remedy lies in the hands of the borrowers.

They would inspire confidence among investors by accepting some form of code of behaviour devised for the protection of private investors in foreign countries. The World Bank is actively engaged in devising such a code which would entail undertaking to submit to the World Bank the arbitrage, or at any rate for conciliation any disputes arising between Governments of debtor countries and their creditors. One of the main difficulties is the reluctance of borrowing Governments to apply some such code not only to new loans but also to the existing capital liabilities to foreign countries.

Since creditors depend on the willingness of sovereign States to honour their obligations or to enable their private citizens to honour theirs, no international agreement can possibly safeguard them adequately. But closer co-operation between lending countries to ensure that if a debtor defaulted on its loan from one country it should be blacklisted in all countries would go some way towards reducing the likelihood of default.

It would greatly assist the expansion of foreign bond issues if the Governments, banks and Stock Exchanges in the countries where the bonds are issued made a real effort to achieve a high degree of unification of their fiscal provisions, exchange restrictions, Stock Exchange practices, legal procedures, etc. As things are, stock arbitrage entails risks even for firms specialising in some transactions, for there is an ever-present possibility that they might not be sufficiently familiar with the laws and practices applied in foreign markets, or that a change in them might have escaped their attention. Discrepancies between laws and practices may be due to differences in their historical evolution, but in many cases it would not be unduly difficult to strike a compromise for the sake of achieving uniformity.

BIBLIOGRAPHY

Bank of England Quarterly Review, 'United Kingdom Overseas Portfolio Investment 1960 to 1962', vol. iii, no. 2, June 1963.

BARLOW, E. R., and WENDER, J., *Profits and Losses on Investment Abroad.* New York, 1955.

CAIRNCROSS, A. K., *Home and Foreign Investment, 1870–1913.* Cambridge, 1953.

COLLIN, F., 'Europe's Unit of Account', *Statist*, February 28, 1964.

Comité chargé d'étudier le financement des investissements, *Rapport présenté au Ministre des Finances et des Affaires Économiques.* Paris, 1963.

Committee on the Working of the Monetary System, *Report* and *Evidence.* London, 1959–60.

DUNNING, J. D., 'Capital Movements in the 20th Century', *Lloyds Bank Review*, April 1964.

Economist, The, 'Where Will All the Borrowers Go ?' August 8, 1964.

EINZIG, PAUL, *The Fight for Financial Supremacy.* London, 1931.

— *A Dynamic Theory of Forward Exchange.* London, 1961.

— *The Euro-Dollar System.* London, 1964.

— The 'European Capital Markets', *The National Banking Review*, June 1964.

FEIS, H., *Europe the World's Banker.* New Haven, 1930.

HOBSON, C. K., *The Export of Capital.* London, 1914.

IVERSEN, CARL, *International Capital Movements.* Copenhagen, 1935.

KENEN, PETER R., 'Towards an Atlantic Capital Market', *Lloyds Bank Review*, April 1964.

KINDLEBERGER, CHARLES P., 'European Economic Integration and the Development of a Single Financial Centre for Long-term Capital', *Weltwirtschaftliches Archiv*, 1963, Heft 2.

LAVINGTON, F., *The English Capital Market.* London, 1921.

LEWIS, C., *America's Stake in International Investment.* Brookings Institute. Washington, 1938.

— *The United States and Foreign Investment Problems.* Washington, 1948.

McMahon, Christopher. *Sterling in the Sixties.* London, 1964.

Macrae, Norman, *The London Capital Market.* London, 1955.

Madden, J. T., and Nadler, Marcus, *The International Money Market.* London, 1935.

Mikesell, R. F. (ed.), *U.S. Private and Government Investment Abroad.* Oregon, 1962.

Myers, Margaret G., *Paris as a Financial Centre.* London, 1936.

Neue Zürcher Zeitung, *Finanzzentren der Welt.* Zürich, 1959.

Nurkse, R., 'The Problem of International Investment Today in the Light of Nineteenth-Century Experience', *Economic Journal,* December 1954.

Rix, M. S., 'The Premium on U.S. Dollar Securities', *Economic Journal,* December 1950.

Royal Institute of International Affairs, *The Problem of International Investments.* London, 1937.

United Nations, *International Capital Movements during the Inter-War Period.* Lake Success, 1949.

— *The International Flow of Private Capital 1946/52.* New York, 1953. *1953/55.* New York, 1956. *1956/58.* New York, 1959.

— *International Flows of Long-term Capital and Official Donations. 1951/59.* New York, 1961. *1959/61,* New York, 1963.

U.S. Treasury, *A Description and Analysis of Certain European Capital Markets.* Joint Economic Committee, U.S. Congress. Washington, 1964.

INDEX